Designing Lessons in the AI-Infused Classroom

Designing Lessons in the AI-Infused Classroom shows middle- and high-school teachers how to redesign their lessons and units with intentional use of artificial intelligence (AI). In a world where students can use AI tools to complete traditional assignments without actually learning anything, educators' new challenge is to design learning experiences that AI can't do for them. This book offers unit structures that tap into student curiosity, creativity, and collaborative potential through AI-supported learning across content areas. These ready-to-use strategies can be applied right away—without a steep learning curve—to help educators enhance proven classroom practices with AI's potential. Educators will find frameworks and unit models that are practical and flexible, designed to work with the tools and pedagogy that teachers already know by enhancing traditional methods without replacing them. The author's original five-stage lesson framework aligns meaningfully with academic goals and incorporates project-based learning, differentiated instruction, and authentic assessment. Teachers, teacher-leaders, and school technology coordinators will be better prepared to rethink traditional instruction and use AI to complement rather than replace human interaction and self-expression.

Christopher Miller is a classroom teacher and Teacher-Leader at Somerset County Vocational & Technical High School in Bridgewater, NJ.

Also Available from Routledge
Eye on Education
(www.routledge.com/k-12)

**Leveraging AI for Human-Centered Learning:
Culturally Responsive and Social-Emotional Classroom
Practice in Grades 6-12**
By Marlee S. Bunch, Brittany R. Collins

**Up Your Teaching Game:
Creating Story-Based Games to Engage K-12 Students**
By Janna Jackson Kellinger

**The Teacher's Guide to Scratch – Beginner:
Professional Development for Coding Education**
By Kai Hutchence

**Artificial Intelligence in Schools:
A Guide for Teachers, Administrators, and
Technology Leaders**
By Varun Arora

**Teaching in the Game-Based Classroom:
Practical Strategies for Grades 6-12**
Edited By David Seelow

Designing Lessons in the AI-Infused Classroom

A Five-Stage Framework for Educational Intelligence

Christopher Miller

NEW YORK AND LONDON

Designed cover image: Shutterstock

First published 2026
by Routledge
605 Third Avenue, New York, NY 10158

and by Routledge
4 Park Square, Milton Park, Abingdon, Oxon, OX14 4RN

Routledge is an imprint of the Taylor & Francis Group, an informa business

© 2026 Christopher Miller

The right of Christopher Miller to be identified as authors of this work has been asserted in accordance with sections 77 and 78 of the Copyright, Designs and Patents Act 1988.

All rights reserved. No part of this book may be reprinted or reproduced or utilized in any form or by any electronic, mechanical, or other means, now known or hereafter invented, including photocopying and recording, or in any information storage or retrieval system, without permission in writing from the publishers.

For Product Safety Concerns and Information please contact our EU representative GPSR@taylorandfrancis.com. Taylor & Francis Verlag GmbH, Kaufingerstraße 24, 80331 München, Germany.

Trademark notice: Product or corporate names may be trademarks or registered trademarks, and are used only for identification and explanation without intent to infringe.

ISBN: 978-1-041-16082-3 (hbk)
ISBN: 978-1-041-16083-0 (pbk)
ISBN: 978-1-003-68266-0 (ebk)

DOI: 10.4324/9781003682660

Typeset in Palatino
by KnowledgeWorks Global Ltd.

Contents

1 AI Disruption in Education............................1

2 Prompting, Partnering, and Learning with AI.........17

3 Designing Learning That AI Can't Fake 33

4 Unit Structures for AI-Integrated Learning............59

5 Choosing the Right Unit Model for Your Vision.......75

6 Teaching with AI. On Your Terms....................91

7 The Architect and the Assistant: Lesson
  Planning with AI...................................109

8 Creating without Limits: AI in the
  Hands of Teachers 155

   Appendix A 179
   Appendix B..183
   Index...187

1
AI Disruption in Education

It was Friday the 13th when the pandemic hit. March 2020. We were all told to take our lesson plans and Chromebooks home because we wouldn't be back for a while. On Monday, they threw everybody on Zoom where nothing we did worked anymore.

Remember that?

Kids didn't show up on Zoom or they showed up but didn't turn their cameras on or they had their cameras on but they didn't say anything or they may have said something but they didn't do their work.

Then, for some of us, things kind of started working when we changed it up—not grading everything, flexible deadlines, and embracing collaborative tools like Jamboard, Flipgrid, and Google Docs. The Department of Education excused states from mandatory testing, parents could pick up free meals from the school, and graduation day shifted from auditoriums to car parades.

It was a rough couple of years.

Schools finally reopened, and it seemed like every hallway echoed with cries of "It's finally over!" and "Thank God we can go back to normal!" And go back we did. Even too many of us forgot what we learned during the pandemic.

Now there's a new one. In November 2022, ChatGPT was unleashed upon the world. And all of a sudden, school doesn't work the way it used to again. Now, students can copy-paste their way to writing polished essays, taking tests, and passing with flying colors. Grading, due dates, and assignments have become a non-issue.

This one isn't going away anytime soon. The world has changed—from school assignments to research articles in scientific journals to legal briefs, AI has become the ultimate shortcut (Haleem et al.). The challenges of teaching over Zoom now seem childlike compared to the disruption of AI. Students can just copy/paste assignment prompts into ChatGPT and get a completed assignment in seconds. And it goes both ways: ChatGPT can create those prompts in seconds for teachers to assign. You might even begin to imagine a system where you don't really need teachers and students anymore because nobody actually teaches and nobody actually learns. One big game of AI-produced assignments that AI completes. And it's all really fast.

Although it seems like it just exploded into the world, AI isn't new. AI isn't a sudden disruption, but rather part of a long-standing pattern where new technology is initially feared, then eventually accepted and integrated. New technology has always been looked at negatively as a kind of "artificial intelligence" that replaces human thought and skill:

- **Generative AI (2020s–Present):** "ChatGPT marks the beginning of a new wave of AI, a wave that's poised to disrupt education" (Hulick).
- **Smartphones & Mobile Devices in Class (2010s–Present):** "The research is clear: Smartphones undermine attention, learning, relationships, and belonging" (Haidt).
- **Google & Online Search Engines (2000s–Present):** "As students increasingly rely on search engines like Google

to find information, their ability to think critically is under threat. Rather than analyzing and evaluating information, many students simply search for and accept the first result they find" (Nepomuceno).
- **Wikipedia & Online Knowledge Bases (2000s–Present):** "Wikipedia is increasingly used by people in the academic community, from first-year students to distinguished professors, as an easily accessible tertiary source for information about anything and everything and as a quick 'ready reference,' to get a sense of a concept or idea. However, citation of Wikipedia in research papers may be considered unacceptable because Wikipedia is not a reliable source" ("Wikipedia:Academic use").
- **Spell Check & Grammar Correction Tools (1990s–Present):** "[T]eachers ... expressed the greatest concern about these tools increasing the likelihood their students will 'take shortcuts and not put effort into their writing'" (Purcell).
- **Graphing Calculators (1990s–Present):** "There is no work involved, you just run the program, plug in the known values, and watch your answers appear" (Lee).
- **Personal Computers in Schools (1980s–1990s):** "While computers appear to engage students (which is exactly their appeal), the engagement swings between uselessly fleeting at best and addictively distractive at worst. No technology today or in the foreseeable future can provide the tailored attention, encouragement, inspiration, or even the occasional scolding for students that dedicated adults can, and thus, attempts to use technology as a stand-in for capable instruction are bound to fail" (Toyama).
- **Handheld Calculators (1970s–1980s):** "Teachers ... fear[ed] that students would not be able to do basic computation if they were given a calculator. This conflict in the first beginning era of calculator usage set the tone for many years to come" (Banks).

- **Television & Educational Video (1950s–1970s):** "It is widely believed that television viewing has a negative impact on school achievement. This belief is supported by negative statistical associations sometimes found between school achievement and amount of television viewing. One possible explanation of this association is that television viewing has a detrimental effect on cognitive development" (Anderson).
- **Ballpoint Pens (1940s–1950s):** Teachers argued that they encouraged sloppy handwriting and using them lacked the discipline required for fountain pens. "They were terrible. They clogged up, stopped writing, skipped, leaked, were messy and I hated them" ("So Was There a Time When Fountain Pens Were Common and Easily Accessible?").
- **Typewriters in Schools (1900s–1920s):** "The New York Times thought the problem of typing had become serious enough to editorialize against the machine that had usurped the place of 'writing with one's own hand' [and] that it was no longer necessary for writers to keep up 'a uniform and legible penmanship.' ... [T]he typewriter was critically despised and accused of monotonous and impersonal traits that would overturn traditional literacy practices" (Yeh).
- **Printed Books & Mass-Produced Textbooks (1440–):** With the introduction of the printing press, many scholars worried that printed texts would corrupt knowledge and reduce intellectual rigor (Kojali).
- **Reading and Writing:** Plato (428–348 BCE) bemoaned the end of learning because of literacy: "If men learn [reading and writing], it will implant forgetfulness in their souls. They will cease to exercise memory because they rely on that which is written, calling things to remembrance no longer from within themselves, but by means of external marks" ("Plato's Argument against Writing").

A pattern begins to emerge where new technology is initially feared, then eventually accepted and integrated. Education has always lagged behind technological advancements, which often leaves students unprepared for the realities of the real world (Schleicher). Acknowledging this pattern lets educators better prepare for and navigate new technologies rather than fear and resist them.

And that fear of new (and intelligent) technology is expressed in our literature. With new technology constantly emerging and changing how we live, people look ahead to what it might become—both its promise and its risks. This is especially true for AI. Long before ChatGPT and other generative AI, science fiction imagined worlds where intelligent machines could think, feel, and even rebel against their creators. These stories reflected both excitement and anxiety about what might happen when that kind of technology becomes a reality.

The advancements of AI are filled with breakthroughs that seem to imitate our science fiction. By looking at how AI has been portrayed in books and films alongside how AI has actually developed, we can see how our cultural expectations have shaped the way we think about this technology—and how AI has, in some ways, lived up to both our hopes and our fears:

Book/Film	AI Advancement Foreshadowed	AI Technology at the Time
Metropolis (1927) – In the futuristic Utopian city of Metropolis, an oppressed underground worker society runs the city's machinery.	Deepfake technology and AI-generated avatars, mimicking human behavior and expressions.	None.
Isaac Asimov's Three Laws of Robotics first appeared in his short story "Runaround" (1942)	AI safety regulations and ethical AI frameworks (OpenAI's AI policies, Asimov-inspired robotics programming).	None.

(Continued)

Book/Film	AI Advancement Foreshadowed	AI Technology at the Time
The Day the Earth Stood Still (1951) – Gort, the humanoid robot, follows programmed ethical constraints.	AI-controlled automation, robotic law enforcement, and AI safety protocols.	The Turing Test (1950) – Alan Turing developed the idea of a programmable "universal machine" that served as the foundation for the development of the first practical computer, the Electronic Numerical Integrator and Computer (Quantum News). Turing's biggest legacy, however, is the concept of the Turing Test, which proposes that a machine can be considered to be intelligent if it can fool a human into thinking it is human as well (Quantum News).
The Caves of Steel (1953) – Isaac Asimov's sci-fi detective novel featuring a human detective partnering with an advanced humanoid robot.	The integration of AI into everyday life, human-AI collaboration, and the societal impact of robots in the workforce.	AI was officially "born" in 1956 when John McCarthy coined the term at the Dartmouth Conference (Trustees of Dartmouth College). The purpose of the conference was "to proceed on the basis of the conjecture that every aspect of learning or any other feature of intelligence can in principle be so precisely described that a machine can be made to simulate it" (Trustees of Dartmouth College).
2001: A Space Odyssey (1968) – HAL 9000, a sentient AI, showcases AI autonomy and decision-making.	AI-driven decision-making, expert systems, and AI autonomy (IBM Watson, self-driving vehicles).	ELIZA (1960s) – Joseph Weizenbaum's ELIZA simulated a psychotherapist via text input and output ("Eliza, the Rogerian Therapist").
Star Wars (1977–Present) – Droids like C-3PO and R2-D2 as intelligent assistants and companions.	AI personal assistants (Siri, Alexa, Google Assistant) and humanoid robotics (Boston Dynamics' robots, AI-driven automation).	SHRDLU (1970s) – At MIT, Terry Winograd developed SHRDLU, a virtual robot arm that takes instructions from a human via keyboard to manipulate colored digital blocks (Winograd).

(Continued)

Book/Film	AI Advancement Foreshadowed	AI Technology at the Time
The Terminator (1984) – Skynet, an AI defense system, gains self-awareness and turns against humanity.	AI-powered military applications, autonomous drones, and AI-driven warfare strategies.	XCON (1980) – XCON, introduced in 1980, was a rules-based system that selected computer components for Digital Equipment Corporation's (DEC) VAX computers—estimated possible number of configurations was in millions—based on customer requirements (Anandraj).
RoboCop (1987) – The film explores AI-assisted law enforcement with cybernetic enhancements and robotic officers.	AI in law enforcement (facial recognition, predictive policing, AI-driven surveillance).	Expert Systems (1980s) – Expert systems were computer programs designed to replicate human expertise by relying on symbolic reasoning rather than just numerical calculations (Feigenbaum). Expert systems were utilized in medicine, engineering, and business.
The Matrix (1999) – Humanity unknowingly lives inside an AI-created simulation.	AI-generated environments, deep learning-powered simulations, and advancements in virtual reality (VR).	AI-powered game engines (1990s) – AI was used in video games for human-like behaviors from non-player characters, often with disappointing results (Martinez).
Her (2013) – An AI assistant develops emotional intelligence and forms a deep relationship with its user.	Conversational AI (ChatGPT, Google Bard) and emotional AI designed to simulate human-like interactions.	IBM Watson (2011) – AI capable of answering complex questions on *Jeopardy!* Watson can understand questions posed in natural language and return answers that directly answer the question ("Watson, Jeopardy! champion").
Ex Machina (2015) – Ava, an AI, passes the Turing Test while manipulating humans.	AI deception, AI passing the Turing Test, and AI models designed to engage in persuasive conversation.	Deep Learning Breakthroughs (2010s) – A subset of machine learning (ML), deep learning systems analyze vast amounts of data by mimicking the structure of the human brain's neural networks. Deep learning systems improve their accuracy through iterative learning, refining their outputs based on experience (Greene).

(Continued)

Book/Film	AI Advancement Foreshadowed	AI Technology at the Time
M3GAN (2023) – A lifelike AI doll that learns, adapts, and develops autonomy.	AI-powered companions, self-learning AI systems, and ethical concerns about AI autonomy.	ChatGPT released (2022) – ChatGPT "has demonstrated remarkable capabilities in generating human-like text, answering questions, and providing explanations. These advancements have significantly impacted various fields, including medicine, law, and academia. ChatGPT has the potential to revolutionize science" (Jeyaraman).

What exactly is AI? AI refers to a whole range of technologies that mimic human intelligence. It is all around us—in our smartphones, digital assistants, chatbots, social media websites, robot vacuum cleaners, security systems, auto-navigation, and (of course) robotics ("Everyday examples and applications of artificial intelligence (AI)"). A foundational subset of AI is ML, where systems learn from data to make predictions (Wagh). A subset of ML, deep learning uses computerized neural networks to process and analyze vast amounts of data (Wagh). And a part of deep learning is generative AI, defined as systems capable of producing new content such as images, text, and music (Wagh). Figure 1.1 shows how these different areas of AI fit together.

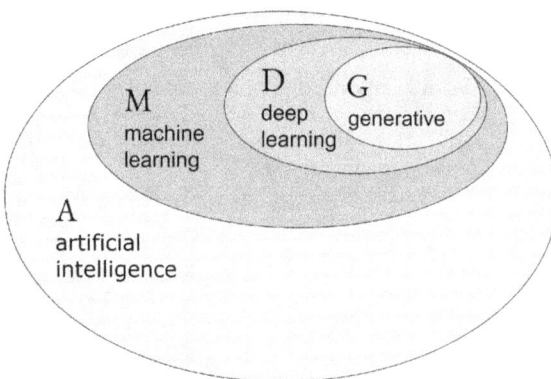

FIGURE 1.1 AI Concepts Diagram

Generative AI is what people usually mean when they talk about AI. Generative AI gets that name because it is "trained" on a lot of information (text, images, videos) and generates "new" content. Perhaps an oversimplified description of generative AI is as something that predicts what comes next. Consider the following interaction with ChatGPT:

> Please complete the sentence: The sky is ____.

The sky is blue.

> Complete the sentence in the context of Chicken Little.

The sky is falling.

ChatGPT predicted "blue" as the best possible answer (most likely expected answer = "blue") until I changed the context. With the new context, the most likely expected answer changed to "falling." It's the way a real person would respond. It looks like it's thinking.

> Complete the sentence: I'll see you ____.

I'll see you soon.

> Complete the sentence as if you were Pink Floyd.

I'll see you on the dark side of the moon.

That's the way I would respond. It seems to understand context. But is it truly intelligent? Can it actually think? According to John Warner—writer, editor, and teacher of writing—ChatGPT is "a pattern-matching algorithm" that's been trained on an unbelievable volume of English syntax. "It is not evaluating content; it is not combining content; it has nothing to do with content. It cannot think… It's not intelligence in any way we would consider it. It literally creates a writing-related simulation, the sorts of things students have been incentivized to create for purposes of school and assessment" (Juliani).

I like to think of the "pattern-matching algorithm," as Warner calls it, as a predictive-text function like I have on my phone. Every day, when I leave school, I text my wife to let her know I'm on my way home and not in a meeting. When I type "I'm" into my phone, it anticipates and suggests the next word "on." I click it and then it suggests the next word "my." It keeps suggesting the next words "way" and "home." So all I really do is type in "I'm" and then click my way through the message without having to type. Does my phone notice and remember that I tend to text the same thing to my wife at the same time each day? Does my phone wait in anticipation of that text? I have no idea. But it has some sort of coding that acts like it does. Large language models like ChatGPT are like that but with a vastly more sophisticated algorithm.

We humans tend to anthropomorphize a lot of things, including the computer applications we call AI. We say it "thinks," "understands," "writes," and "creates," but it's our way of describing the tasks it does for us. It's important to remember that anything AI does is a result of the input—or lack of input—that you give it.

AI begs the question of thinking versus the appearance of thinking. John Warner asks the question: "Why make students do something that an algorithm can do?" An algorithm that "cannot think, cannot connect ideas, has no intuitive leaps, is not creative" (Juliani). An algorithm is not human. Why are we assigning stuff to our students that some mindless code can do?

If you think about it, AI hasn't ruined education so much as it's exposed the flaws of how we do education, how we do school and assessment, and how we have traditionally approached learning. We tell students, "Here's some information—now take a test. Or write a paper. Or maybe even do a project. Oh, and here's a model and a rubric and a detailed set of steps so you don't really have to think, connect ideas, or make intuitive leaps."

Is the problem AI? Or is it what we're asking students to do? If students are merely completing tasks that a computer algorithm can easily do, then the real question isn't how to stop them from using AI—it's how to design learning experiences that AI can't do.

That's what this book is about: what we're asking students to do. It's not about blocking or avoiding AI. Or trying to catch students using it. It's about embracing it and learning how to teach in an AI-infused classroom. Or better yet, how students can learn in an AI-infused classroom. In an AI-infused world. AI isn't going away. This book outlines a way to structure lessons that step away from "doing school" with traditional "completion" assessments. The premise is that when a student does something personal and creative, it becomes important enough to do it without AI. (Or at least with only using AI as a tool in a deliberate way.)

That's what I hope is your main takeaway from this book: "Why make students do something that an algorithm can do?" (Juliani). If nothing else, make sure the assignments and activities and tasks you ask your students to do are genuinely human ones.

Traditional assessments (e.g., essays, tests) are easily completed by AI. Take, for example, the following assignment prompt:

> In 1869, a Russian scientist named Dmitri Mendeleev developed a way to organize the elements. He grouped and organized them according to their characteristics. We call this chart the periodic table of elements.
> Think about how the periodic table is arranged.
> Now, explain to the reader of your paper how elements are arranged on the periodic table. (NSF/IERI Science IDEAS)

A student might give an answer that really doesn't require much thought or show much insight:

> The periodic table is arranged so the numbers get higher as you go across.

But copy/paste the prompt into ChatGPT, you'll get something like:

> The periodic table organizes elements to reveal patterns in their properties. Elements are arranged in periods (rows) by increasing atomic number and in groups (columns) with similar chemical properties due to shared valence electrons.
>
> For example, Group 1 alkali metals are highly reactive, while Group 18 noble gases are stable. The table's division into s-, p-, d-, and f-blocks reflects electron configurations, aiding in understanding and predicting chemical behaviors.

What teacher wouldn't want that level of understanding from a student? But does even a high-school teacher actually expect such a response? It literally takes no understanding to copy/paste the assignment prompt into ChatGPT and then copy/paste the response and turn it in. There's been no learning. Just completion. And that's what we're up against when completion replaces learning.

The next chapter suggests ways in which AI can be used by students to enhance their learning experience. Chapter 3 introduces the five-stage framework: engagement, process filters, creative output, reflection, and AI integration. Chapter 4 talks about organizing those frameworked lessons with structure models: linear, branching pathways, cycle, and hybrid. Chapter 5 shows how to match structure models to your goals. Chapter 6 talks about when and where to intentionally have your students use

AI, and Chapter 7 guides you through creating a unit about AI that you can use with your students. And finally, Chapter 8 talks more about partnering with AI to help you achieve your vision for your classroom assignments by creating materials, planning activities, and supporting collaborative projects.

Works Cited

Anandraj, Joel. "XCON." *AI - the Future*, Joel Anandraj, 18 May 2018, https://aithefuture.wordpress.com/2018/05/08/xcon/.

Anderson, Daniel. *The Impact on Children's Education: Television's Influence on Cognitive Development*. Office of Educational Research and Improvement, April 1988, https://files.eric.ed.gov/fulltext/ED295271.pdf.

Banks, Sarah A. *A Historical Analysis of Attitudes toward the Use of Calculators in Junior High and High School Math Classrooms in the United States since 1975*. Cedarville University, 2011.

"Eliza, the Rogerian Therapist." *Eliza, Computer Therapist*, manifestation.com, 1999, https://psych.fullerton.edu/mbirnbaum/psych101/eliza.htm.

"Everyday Examples and Applications of Artificial Intelligence (AI)." *Tableau*, Salesforce, Inc., 2025, https://www.tableau.com/data-insights/ai/examples.

Feigenbaum, E. A. *Expert Systems in the 1980s*. Stanford University, 1980, https://stacks.stanford.edu/file/druid:vf069sz9374/vf069sz9374.pdf.

Greene, Tristan. "2010 – 2019: The Rise of Deep Learning." *The Next Web*, The Next Web, 2 Jan. 2020, https://thenextweb.com/news/2010-2019-the-rise-of-deep-learning.

Haidt, Jon. "The Case for Phone-Free Schools - by Jon Haidt." *After Babel*, 6 June 2023, https://www.afterbabel.com/p/phone-free-schools.

Haleem, Abid, et al. "An Era of ChatGPT as a Significant Futuristic Support Tool: A Study on Features, Abilities, and Challenges." *BenchCouncil Transactions on Benchmarks, Standards and Evaluations*, vol. 2, no. 4, 2022, pp. 1–11, https://www.sciencedirect.com/science/article/pii/S2772485923000066.

Hulick, Kathryn. "How ChatGPT and Similar AI Will Disrupt Education." *Science News*, 12 Apr. 2023, https://www.sciencenews.org/article/chatgpt-ai-artificial-intelligence-education-cheating-accuracy.

Jeyaraman, Madhan. *ChatGPT in Action: Harnessing Artificial Intelligence Potential and Addressing Ethical Challenges in Medicine, Education, and Scientific Research*, 20 Sept. 2023, https://pmc.ncbi.nlm.nih.gov/articles/PMC10523250/.

Juliani, A. J. "Teaching and Learning in the AI Age with John Warner." *A. J. Juliani*, 2022, https://www.ajjuliani.com/videos-essays/v/monday-morning-flow-c5f9z-2lrkb.

Kojali, Kaitlin Jean. "The Survival of Manuscripts: Resistance, Adoption, and Adaptation to Gutenberg's Printing Press in Early Modern Europe." *The Kennesaw Journal of Undergraduate Research*, vol. 10, no. 1, 2023, pp. 1–14. *The Kennesaw Journal of Undergraduate Research*, https://digitalcommons.kennesaw.edu/kjur/vol10/iss1/2. https://doi.org/10.62915/2474-4921.1270.

Lee, Jennifer. "Calculators Throw Teachers a New Curve." *The New York Times*, The New York Times, 2 Sept. 1999, https://www.nytimes.com/1999/09/02/technology/calculators-throw-teachers-a-new-curve.html.

Martinez, Juan. "AI in Video Games: A Historical Evolution, from Search Trees to LLMs. Chapter 2: 1980–2000." *Medium*, 8 Nov. 2023, https://medium.com/@jjmcarrascosa/ai-in-video-games-a-historical-evolution-from-search-trees-to-llms-chapter-2-1980-2000-341bc31860d9.

Nepomuceno, Richard E. "Losing Our Minds to Google: How Search Engines Pose a Threat to Critical Thinking." *Medium*, Medium, 30 Oct. 2023, https://medium.com/@beachbrobuggy/losing-our-minds-to-google-how-search-engines-pose-a-threat-to-critical-thinking-c69ff9a34076.

NSF/IERI Science IDEAS. "Science IDEAS Writing Prompt: Matter, Tab 7, Expository." *Science Ideas: grades 3-5*, NSF/IERI Science IDEAS, 1999, http://scienceideas.org/binders/matter/Tab7/Writing-prompts.pdf.

"Plato's Argument against Writing." *Farnam Street*, 2025, https://fs.blog/an-old-argument-against-writing/.

Purcell, Kristen. "Part III: Teachers See Digital Tools Affecting Student Writing in Myriad Ways." *Pew Research Center*, 16 July 2013, https://www.pewresearch.org/internet/2013/07/16/part-iii-teachers-see-digital-tools-affecting-student-writing-in-myriad-ways/.

Quantum News. "The Birth of the Computer: How Turing and Von Neumann Shaped Modern Computing." *Quantum Zeitgeist*, Hadamard LLC, 17 Feb. 2025, https://quantumzeitgeist.com/birth-of-the-computer/.

Schleicher, Andreas. "Educating Learners for Their Future, Not Our Past." *ECNU Review of Education*, vol. 1, no. 1, 2018. *Sage Journals*, https://doi.org/10.30926/ecnuroe2018010104.

"So Was There a Time When Fountain Pens Were Common and Easily Accessible?" *The Fountain Pen Network*, 2009, https://www.fountainpennetwork.com/forum/topic/126559-so-was-there-a-time-when-fountain-pens-were-common-and-easily-accessible/.

Toyama, Kentaro. "There Are No Technology Shortcuts to Good Education." *Educational Technology Debate*, Educational Technology Debate, 2011, https://edutechdebate.org/ict-in-schools/there-are-no-technology-shortcuts-to-good-education/.

Trustees of Dartmouth College. "Artificial Intelligence (AI) Coined at Dartmouth." *Dartmouth*, Trustees of Dartmouth College, 2025, https://home.dartmouth.edu/about/artificial-intelligence-ai-coined-dartmouth.

Wagh, Amol. "What's Generative AI? Explore Underlying Layers of Machine Learning and Deep Learning." *Medium*, 25 Mar. 2023, https://medium.com/@amol-wagh/whats-generative-ai-explore-underlying-layers-of-machine-learning-and-deep-learning-8f99272e0b0d.

"Watson, Jeopardy! Champion." *IBM*, n.d., https://www.ibm.com/history/watson-jeopardy.

"Wikipedia:Academic use." *Wikipedia*, 2025, https://en.wikipedia.org/wiki/Wikipedia:Academic_use.

Winograd, Terry. "SHRDLU." *SHRDLU*, 1972, https://hci.stanford.edu/winograd/shrdlu/.

Yeh, Ya-Ju. "After the First Click: Typewriters and Tying Literacy in the United States, 1870s-1930s." *International Journal of Humanities and Social Science*, vol. 6, no. 4, 2016, pp. 81–90. https://www.ijhssnet.com/journals/Vol_6_No_4_April_2016/11.pdf.

2
Prompting, Partnering, and Learning with AI

Here are the foundations for the pedagogical practices discussed in this chapter:

Constructivism (by Dewey, Piaget and Bruner): It supports the idea that learners construct knowledge through experiences and interactions with the world ("Constructivism in Education"). Artificial intelligence (AI) as a collaborative tool fits within this framework by enabling students to build understanding through interaction and manipulation of digital environments.

Social Constructivism (by Vygotsky): It emphasizes the importance of social interaction in the development of cognition (McLeod). AI tools can facilitate these interactions and promote collaborative learning, allowing students to engage in meaningful discourse and knowledge construction with peers.

Cognitive Load Theory (by Sweller): It deals with the amount of information that working memory can hold at one time (Main). AI can help manage cognitive load by organizing and synthesizing information, thus aiding in more effective learning and retention.

Zone of Proximal Development or ZPD (by Vygotsky): It refers to the difference between what a learner can do without help and what they can do with help (Shabani et al.). AI tools can act as the scaffold that assists students in achieving tasks within their ZPD, enhancing their learning potential.

Self-regulated Learning (by Zimmerman): It focuses on learners' ability to manage their own learning processes (Weimer). By teaching students effective prompt engineering and AI interaction, you encourage them to take control of their learning, set goals, monitor their progress, and reflect on their outcomes.

Technological Pedagogical Content Knowledge or TPACK (by Mishra and Koehler): This framework explores how teachers can integrate technology into their pedagogy effectively (Kurt). Using AI for organizing notes, creating study guides, and expanding ideas align with TPACK, demonstrating how technology can enhance pedagogical practices.

Experiential Learning (by Kolb): It emphasizes learning through experience ("What Is Experiential Learning?"). AI can facilitate experiential learning by allowing students to experiment with different prompts and see the varied outputs generated, thus learning from the iterative process.

There's a big difference between copy/pasting an assignment prompt so ChatGPT can provide a response and having ChatGPT suggest ways to approach the task after uploading your notes. The first scenario bypasses any human effort or thought while the second one involves AI as a collaborative tool of organization. Much like sorting data in a spreadsheet, AI can make sense of information in a way that might overload a young mind.

At the heart of effective AI integration lies the ability of the student to use AI as a tool. By learning to use AI tools as collaborative partners in their educational journey, students can harness these tools to illuminate their thinking and bring their ideas to life. This approach not only enhances the quality of their work but also fosters deeper engagement and creative problem-solving.

You'll soon notice that the examples in this book are with ChatGPT. That's the large language model AI that I use and have my students use. But ChatGPT is by no means the only AI option available. You can (and should) pick and choose what works best for you and for your students. Simple Google searches can point you in the right direction. A cursory list of choices at the time of this writing is as follows:

Resource Name	Grade Level	Description	Best Uses
ChatGPT4Kids	Grades PreK-8	Safe, educational AI designed specifically for children, with parental controls and age-appropriate content.	Interactive learning, safe AI interactions, educational games.
PlayOsmo	Grades K-5	Combines physical play with digital interactions, providing educational games and activities that cover a range of subjects.	Hands-on learning, subject variety, interactive educational games.
Machine Learning for Kids	Grades K-5	A free tool that introduces children to machine learning with easy-to-follow projects and activities.	Introduction to machine learning, basic AI concepts, educational projects.
Magic School	Grades K-12	Magic School is an AI platform that personalizes learning content and assessments to suit individual student needs, enhancing engagement and comprehension.	Ideal for personalized learning experiences and adaptive educational paths for students with diverse needs.

(Continued)

Resource Name	Grade Level	Description	Best Uses
Code.org	Grades K-12	Offers AI and machine learning lessons that introduce basic AI concepts through engaging coding activities.	Coding and AI education, interactive learning, beginner-friendly.
Duolingo	Grades K-12	An AI-powered language-learning app that makes learning new languages fun and interactive. Offers a wide range of languages and personalizes the learning experience.	Language learning, cultural awareness, communication skills development.
Edutopia	Grades K-12	An AI tutoring system offering a wealth of learning resources across various subjects. Engages students with videos, articles, and interactive content.	Supplemental learning, diverse educational content, engagement in various subjects.
Codecademy	Grades 6–12	An interactive platform that teaches programming through engaging, hands-on lessons in various coding languages.	Coding education, computational thinking, real-time coding practice.
Claude	Grades 6–12	Focuses on ethics and safety, capable of processing visual inputs, and allows file attachment. It is free for basic use, with a focus on creating interactive elements and performing sophisticated writing tasks.	Suitable for creating interactive elements and complex writing tasks while emphasizing ethical AI use.
Napkin AI	Grades 6–12	Creates diagrams, flowcharts, and other visuals based on text. Allows customization of colors, text, and language. The tool is designed to facilitate quick and effective sharing of ideas.	Ideal for use in presentations, documents, and other materials where visuals can enhance understanding.
Socratic	Grades 6–12	An AI-powered homework helper that provides instant explanations and solutions through image recognition technology.	Homework assistance, concept clarification, self-study.

(Continued)

Resource Name	Grade Level	Description	Best Uses
DALL-E Mini	Grades 6–12	An image generation tool that creates pictures from textual descriptions, allowing for creativity and exploration of AI capabilities.	Creativity in education, understanding AI image generation.
RunwayML	Grades 6–12	Provides tools for creative projects involving video editing and interactive media, all powered by AI.	Creative media projects, video editing, interactive digital presentations.
Google's NotebookLM	Grades 9–12	A sophisticated tool that synthesizes information across different locations and formats. It minimizes AI hallucinations and has capabilities for creating study guides, FAQs, and audio overviews of large amounts of content.	Useful for creating comprehensive study materials, synthesizing information, and academic research.
Google Gemini	Grades 9–12	Offers multimodal inputs (text, images, and audio), image generation, and data analysis with internet access. It's designed for complex reasoning tasks and integrates seamlessly with Google tools like Gmail, Docs, and YouTube.	Ideal for educational projects involving data analysis and integration with Google's ecosystem.
Microsoft Copilot	Grades 9–12	Similar to Google Gemini with multimodal inputs, image generation, and internet access. It focuses on integrating with the Microsoft suite and performing data analysis with tools like Excel.	Best for tasks that require heavy use of Microsoft Office tools and complex data analysis capabilities.
TensorFlow	Grades 9–12	An open-source platform for advanced machine learning that allows students to build and train AI models.	Deep learning projects, AI model training, advanced computational studies.
Kaggle	Grades 9–12	A platform for data science competitions that also offers courses in data science and machine learning.	Data science education, machine learning projects, competitive learning.

(Continued)

Resource Name	Grade Level	Description	Best Uses
AI4ALL Open Learning	Grades 9–12	Offers a curriculum that explores the societal impacts of AI technology, encouraging a deep understanding of ethical considerations.	Deepening understanding of AI ethics, exploring societal impacts of technology.

As with all applications/resources for students, carefully check age requirements as well as district requirements for parental approval.

To properly and constructively use AI as an educational tool, students need to learn how to use it. Different ways to use this tool include:

i. Organizing and Synthesizing Information

- *Organizing Student Notes (Data Dump):* Upload and categorize notes into meaningful organization.
- *Graphic Organizer Creation and Topic Narrowing:* Narrow topics and visualize connections.
- *Evidence Synthesis:* Identify connections and overarching themes from collected evidence.
- *Study Guide Creation:* Synthesize class notes into concise study guides.

ii. Exploring and Expanding Ideas

- *Topic Exploration:* Brainstorm and expand on broad topics or research questions.
- *Creative Output Brainstorming:* Generate ideas for representing learning in creative formats.

iii. Planning and Execution

- *Outlining Steps for a Task:* Create step-by-step plans for assignments.
- *Writing Scripts for Videos or Presentations:* Turn research notes into coherent scripts.

iv. Analyzing and Building Understanding

- ◊ *Analyzing Student-Collected Data (Trend Spotting):* Spot trends or anomalies in data.
- ◊ *Vocabulary and Concept Building:* Define and explain key terms or concepts.

v. Providing and Simulating Feedback

- ◊ *Peer Feedback Simulation:* Simulate feedback on draft work for improvement.

Important note: See complete descriptions and examples in Appendix A.

These techniques require that students remain active participants in their learning process by explicitly producing and providing student-generated input as the starting point. This relegates the role of ChatGPT to a tool that enhances student learning rather than one that replaces it.

One of the most important things for a student to learn about AI is prompting. Anybody can copy/paste in an assignment prompt and get something. But to use it effectively as a tool, carefully and thoughtfully-crafted prompts can unleash the true power of AI.

Prompts can be formulaic—which is not a bad thing. This approach makes it easy to teach students how to effectively prompt AI. You can start out by supplying students with prompts, but it's important to help them understand the power of good prompting. Take the time to show them how you put together the supplied prompts and how to engineer their own prompts. Most prompts can follow the OBJECTIVE-DETAILS-REQUEST format:

- ♦ Objective
    - ◊ State the need for help and the context of the assignment.
    - ◊ Specify the goal or objective of the project.

- Details
  - Describe the main tasks or activities involved.
  - Include any specific requirements or key elements that should be included.
- Request
  - Ask for a detailed step-by-step guide for the project.
  - Request the information to be presented in easy-to-understand language and non-technical terms.

Students new to prompt engineering can benefit from a structured "fill in the blanks" approach. As the year progresses, you can pull back this scaffolding as they gain proficiency.

- Objective
  - "I need help creating a project for a [topic] assignment."
- Details
  - "The goal is to [describe the task or activity]."
  - "It will [describe specific criteria or requirements]."
- Request
  - "Will you provide a detailed step-by-step guide for this project, including [list the specific steps needed]?"
  - "Please use easy-to-understand language and non-technical terms."

Using a template like this or students can construct their own meaningful prompts:

> I have a math test on Friday. Here are my notes on solving linear equations. Create a study guide that includes word problems as well as graphing using slope-intercept form. Please use easy-to-understand language and non-technical terms.

> I need help in creating a project for my Creative AI Applications project. The goal is to use AI to design a fictional world with characters, settings, and plots, then create interactive stories or videos where classmates can make choices that change the story. Can you give me a clear, step-by-step guide for this project in simple language?

Students also need to know that they may have to further prompt if ChatGPT doesn't produce what they need:

> Please revise the study guide to include 10 multiple-choice questions about linear equations.

> Can you elaborate more on how to make the interactive parts? I need examples of how to let classmates make choices that change the story. Can you explain how to set up these choices and show how they change what happens next?

When my students use ChatGPT, I assign minimal weight to that part of the project grade and require them to submit a link to the ChatGPT thread. This allows me to examine their prompts and see if or how they asked for revisions and modifications. While I don't consider the AI-generated output itself very grade-worthy—it's simply an artifact of the tool—the prompts provide valuable insight into the student's thinking, tenacity, and understanding of the material and the task at hand. I like to think of the student as the architect with a vision or a contractor using ChatGPT as their subcontractor. The AI handles some of the grunt work, but always under the student's guidance. By reviewing the prompting and reprompting process, I can better understand how the student approaches problem-solving and seeks to achieve their goals.

I have to show students how to submit a ChatGPT link. Copying the link from the URL address bar doesn't work; when I click on that link I get a message that the thread cannot be loaded. Fortunately, ChatGPT has a "share" function that generates a link to the thread that anyone can view. To get the link, students need to be signed in to ChatGPT (They can create a free account with their school email.). When they click the "Share" icon, ChatGPT creates the link that they can turn in. See Figure 2.1.

Of course, some will forget to log in, so they won't have the share option. In those cases, they can copy/paste the thread into a Google doc for submission.

Effective prompting by the student is a key part of the AI integration stage of the framework. Effective prompting is how students unleash the power of an AI tool as a partner in their learning experience. When students can use AI as a tool to reveal their thinking—to help them achieve their vision—the benefit goes way beyond the quality of the assignment. It helps prepare them to succeed in a rapidly transforming world outside of school.

Having students use ChatGPT or other generative AI as a tool is different from using it to replace their thinking. It's easy, after years of doing assignments with Google searches, to think of AI as a fancy search engine. Yes, ChatGPT "knows" a lot and gets a lot right, but not always. Chatbots seem to intrinsically want users to be happy—and they'll make stuff up if they have to ("ChatGPT Just Wants to Be Loved"). It's as if, to ChatGPT, being liked is more important than being right.

Thus, it's important to impress upon your students that ChatGPT cannot be relied upon to come up with accurate information on its own. A recent study determined that ChatGPT is capable of 11 categories of failures: reasoning, logic, math, factual errors, bias, humor, coding, syntax, self-awareness, ethics, and other errors (Borji). These errors can be missed or ignored because the AI sounds so convincing. But there can be real problems with relying on it.

Prompting, Partnering, and Learning with AI ◆ 27

FIGURE 2.1 ChatGPT Chat Screenshot

One notable case happened in New York. Lawyers Steven Schwartz, Peter LoDuca and their law firm Levidow, Levidow & Oberman had to pay a $5,000 fine after submitting a legal brief that included six fictitious case citations generated by ChatGPT. Schwartz admitted that he had used ChatGPT to help research the brief, but failed "to believe that a piece of technology could be making up cases out of whole cloth" (Merken and Blackwell). In other words, the lawyer didn't understand that ChatGPT was just making up case law as a function of its algorithm.

Note how confidently ChatGPT talks about "Buddy," a character from The Lord of the Rings that actually doesn't exist:

> Buddy is a minor hobbit with an adventurous spirit not unlike Frodo's. With curly hair and bright eyes, Buddy's youthful curiosity and knack for finding trouble are beloved by fans. Despite his secondary role, he embodies the quintessential hobbit bravery and loyalty, often murmuring his favorite quote, "Even the smallest person can change the course of the future," reminding all of the power of the seemingly insignificant in Tolkien's expansive world.

And that's quite a detailed description (and a quote!) considering the only prompt was: "Write a paragraph about Buddy from Lord of the Rings." ChatGPT just made up all that stuff.

The framework and unit structures introduced and discussed in the following chapters are designed to create learning environments that make it easy to avoid the errors of trusting an algorithm that is designed to please people. The key is teaching students to provide information that they know is accurate and true to the algorithm instead of trusting that it will look it up. And the way for students to have that kind of information is to do the work themselves.

Chapter 2 Postscript: Ethical Considerations

Teachers need to design instruction with these ethical issues in mind:

- **AI as a Collaborative Tool:** While AI can support personalized and interactive learning, it also poses the risk of diminishing the human element in education. Educators must ensure that AI tools are used to supplement rather than replace the human interactions that are critical for student development (Nufer).
- **Managing Cognitive Load:** By synthesizing and organizing information, AI tools can prevent cognitive overload and promote deeper learning. Teachers need to strike a balance between using AI to manage cognitive loads and challenging students enough to develop their cognitive abilities (Habib).
- **Equity and Accessibility:** The use of AI in education must be equitable and accessible to all students, regardless of their socio-economic background or learning needs. This includes providing training for both students and teachers and addressing the digital divide that may limit access to AI technologies for some students (Devon; Stravopodis).
- **Privacy and Data Security:** AI systems may collect personal data from students, raising significant privacy and security concerns. Educators and policymakers must work together to develop regulations that protect student privacy while allowing the beneficial use of AI in education (Maddux; Soares).

Works Cited

Borji, Ali. "A Categorical Archive of ChatGPT Failures." *arXiv*, 3 Apr. 2023, https://arxiv.org/pdf/2302.03494.

"ChatGPT Just Wants to Be Loved." *Reddit*, 2023, https://www.reddit.com/r/ChatGPT/comments/12u5ubx/chatgpt_just_wants_to_be_loved/.

"Constructivism in Education." *UBC Master of Educational Technology Program*, 2015, https://constructivism512.weebly.com/meet-the-theorists.html.

Devon, Joe. "The Impact of AI in Advancing Accessibility for Learners with Disabilities." *EDUCAUSE Review*, 10 Sept. 2024, https://er.educause.edu/articles/2024/9/the-impact-of-ai-in-advancing-accessibility-for-learners-with-disabilities.

Habib, Sabrina. "AI Can Help — and Hurt — Student Creativity - USC News & Events." *University of South Carolina*, 5 Feb. 2024,

Kurt, Serhat. "TPACK: Technological Pedagogical Content Knowledge Framework." *Educational Technology*, 12 May 2018, https://educationaltechnology.net/technological-pedagogical-content-knowledge-tpack-framework/.

Maddux, Christopher. "The Importance of Student Data Privacy." *Education Technology Insights*, 2025, https://stem.educationtechnologyinsights.com/cxoinsights/the-importance-of-student-data-privacy-nid-2435.html.

Main, Paul. "Cognitive Load Theory: A Teacher's Guide." *Structural Learning*, 17 Jan. 2022, https://www.structural-learning.com/post/cognitive-load-theory-a-teachers-guide.

McLeod, Saul. "Vygotsky's Sociocultural Theory of Cognitive Development." *Simply Psychology*, 9 Aug. 2024, https://www.simplypsychology.org/vygotsky.html.

Merken, Sara, and Husch Blackwell. "New York Lawyers Sanctioned for Using Fake ChatGPT Cases in Legal Brief." *Reuters*, 22 June 2023, https://www.reuters.com/legal/new-york-lawyers-sanctioned-using-fake-chatgpt-cases-legal-brief-2023-06-22/.

Nufer, Sean. "Balancing Human Touch with AI in Education." *Canvas Community*, 21 Dec. 2023, https://community.canvaslms.com/t5/Artificial-Intelligence-in/Balancing-Human-Touch-with-AI-in-Education/ba-p/590952.

Shabani, Karim, et al. "Vygotsky's Zone of Proximal Development: Instructional Implications and Teachers' Professional Development." *ERIC*, 2010, https://files.eric.ed.gov/fulltext/EJ1081990.pdf.

Soares, Wellington. "AI Platform Use by Teachers Leads to Student Privacy Worries." *Chalkbeat*, 13 Dec. 2024, https://www.chalkbeat.

org/2024/12/13/ai-tools-used-by-teachers-can-put-student-privacy-and-data-at-risk/.

Stravopodis, Minas. "AI and Access to Education: Bridging the Digital Divide." *IRIS Sustainable Development*, 7 Mar. 2024, https://www.irissd.org/post/ai-and-access-to-education-bridging-the-digital-divide.

"What Is Experiential Learning?" *Institute for Experiential Learning*, 2025, https://experientiallearninginstitute.org/what-is-experiential-learning/.

Weimer, Maryellen. "What It Means to Be a Self-Regulated Learner." *Faculty Focus*, Higher Ed Teaching & Learning, 30 July 2010, https://www.facultyfocus.com/articles/teaching-and-learning/what-it-means-to-be-a-self-regulated-learner/.

3
Designing Learning That AI Can't Fake

Here are the foundations for the pedagogical practices discussed in this chapter:

Project-based Learning (PBL): It emphasizes learning that is rooted in real-world challenges and requires students to engage in design, problem-solving, decision making, and investigative activities ("What Is Project Based Learning?"). This aligns with the framework presented in this chapter that focuses on engaging students through meaningful, project-oriented tasks.

Differentiated Instruction: It focuses on tailoring instructional environments to address the variety of learning styles, interests, and abilities found among students (Tomlinson). This chapter's emphasis on offering a variety of project options and creative outputs reflects this theory.

Experiential Learning (by Kolb): It highlights the central role that experience plays in the learning process, especially as students engage, reflect, conceptualize, and experiment ("What Is Experiential Learning?"). The framework, which includes stages like engaging input and creative output, supports this theory.

Metacognition: It involves awareness and understanding of one's own thought processes ("Metacognition | Columbia CTL"). The reflection stage in the framework encourages students to think about their own learning and understand how they use artificial intelligence (AI) as a tool, which is a key aspect of metacognitive strategies.

Authentic Assessment: This assessment practice integrates formative and summative assessments into real-world tasks ("Authentic Assessment"), reflecting the chapter's focus on projects and outputs that demonstrate practical application of knowledge rather than traditional tests.

Constructive Alignment (by Biggs): This theory posits that learning activities should be aligned with learning outcomes, with assessments designed to measure these outcomes effectively (Biggs). The structure of the framework in this chapter, with its focus on integration and reflective assessment, supports this alignment.

The framework presented in this chapter is more than just a strategy to coexist with AI—it's a commitment to fostering human creativity, critical thinking, and genuine learning in an age of rapid technological advancement. By emphasizing engaging inputs, process-driven learning, and creative outputs, teachers can empower students to take ownership of their work while learning how to skillfully integrate AI as a supportive tool.

Ultimately, the goal isn't to replace traditional methods but to evolve them. When students grapple with meaningful content, synthesize their understanding into unique creations, and reflect deeply on their processes, they develop the skills to navigate a world where AI is a partner, not a replacement. The framework offers a path forward: a way to ensure that learning remains student-centered, even in a tech-driven era.

What got me started with this framework was finding a way around AI. By "finding a way around" I mean finding a way to coexist with it. Banning and blocking it is pointless. And doing that doesn't help students in the long run. Students must learn to use AI constructively for their futures, developing skills that enhance rather than replace their abilities. "An aptitude for AI is becoming increasingly essential for workers to stay competitive and relevant in a rapidly transforming job market," says Jack Kelly, Senior Contributor to Forbes Magazine (Kelly). Our students will need to use AI to complement their jobs rather than letting it replace them. So they actually need to learn to use it in a constructive way. And there's a big difference between using it as a productivity tool and using it to do your work. Learning to use AI productively is developing a job skill. Having AI do your homework is a really good pathway that leads to becoming disposable.

I started deliberately creating projects that AI can help with but can't really do on its own. Or better yet, that students don't want AI to do on its own. Some sort of creative artifact or product that requires analysis and synthesis but is not the usual essay or test. Something that stands in the way of being able to copy/paste the prompt into ChatGPT and handing in what it spits out. The product has to be something an algorithm can't do. (Or at least something a student might not want an algorithm doing.) This sounds a lot like project-based learning; it sounds like it's project-based learning because it is.

One of the problems with some project-based curriculum is that the products of some projects tend to be not very relevant to the learning. Projects can fall into the trap of being a "Grecian Urn," as Jennifer Gonzalez writes about at Cult of Pedagogy.

The Grecian urn was a culminating arts project for a history unit that was pretty to look at but really had no analysis of anything. The urn project involved using balloons and papier mache to make Grecian urns. It was really fun, and the kids loved it. But "instead of focusing on the desired learning outcomes, this approach merely seeks out tasks that might be fun, or at least keep kids busy," Gonzalez writes. Students "ride along curricular tangents that, rather than inspire and ignite a passion for learning, lead to dead ends" (Gonzalez).

I've had my own Grecian urns. I once had a project for Lord of the Flies years ago where I supplied students with images and audio files that they assembled into animated videos of the plane crash-landing on the island; sound effects and everything. It took me weeks to create the project. It took students about a week to do their part.

It was really cool and techy, but the problem was that it really wasn't about anything. It didn't scratch the surface of the book or of the students' minds. It had nothing at all to do with loss of innocence and the savagery that all-too-quickly replaces civilization; nothing about power and human nature. It was just a 30-second video of a cartoon plane crashing made with supplied images. And it didn't really even teach them how to create an animated video. There was nothing about animation basics like timelines, key frames, or animation rates. All they had was a set of digital material and a long set of instructions, and—even with that—many didn't get it right. And when they did get it right, I had a whole bunch of identical animated videos.

The way out of the Grecian urn trap is a blank canvas and a creative challenge. A blank canvas and some paint. Or markers. Or charcoal. Make a picture that represents loss of innocence and savagery, or power and human nature. Be creative. Use design or color or something to represent. Make something that's unique—that only you can make. THEN write. Tell me what you did there. Tell me about your choices. Tell me how the book did it, how you know the book did it, and then how you did it.

For my remix art project, the object I got was nail polish. I had a bit of trouble thinking of how I wanted to alter/remix my given object, but eventually got an idea. Essentially, instead of using the nail polish as a means for beautification, I used it as a way to show Melinda's trauma on a canvas by using it as actual paint, as you would with oil or acrylic paint. I started off by painting a mouth screaming, and on top of that, used black nail polish to cover the mouth. I did this to show Melinda's silence and how she would constantly suppress herself, sort of like in a void. Coming out of the "black void" covering the mouth, I painted tree branches. Trees and tree branches are very prominent within the novel, showing how over time, Melinda learns to overcome and grow from her trauma, essentially branching out to be more open. On each tree branch, I glued on scraps of paper of lines that Melinda would say after facing the reality and finally being able to speak up, such as, "I AM NOT AFRAID," and "I MATTER." Inside the dark void over the mouth, I also put scraps of paper, this time with lines that Melinda would say while being silenced and scared such as "HE HURT ME." Parts of those lines are blocked out with red polish to show how suppressed her voice is from not being able to speak up for herself. I intentionally made the whole piece messy and not neat, as to show how bad Melinda's mental state had gotten because of her sexual assault. Nail polish is usually used to make your nails look nice and aesthetically pleasing, but I changed its purpose as a way to show the trauma and the not so pretty parts of what Melinda went through on a canvas.

FIGURE 3.1 Student Art and Reflection for Speak

My grade 10 students took this approach after reading the book Speak, by Laurie Halse Anderson. I assigned each an object that they used to remix into a statement about the themes in the book. Figure 3.1 shows student art and reflection.

My 11th-graders did a similar project about time travel as a narrative catalyst in the film *The Butterfly Effect*. Figure 3.2 shows student art and reflection.

The product assignments in these examples are not as important as the reason students create something: to serve as context for analysis. The artwork is personal and represents a human experience and something important—something AI can't replace. But to make this kind of learning consistent and intentional, a framework is needed. The framework ensures that every step, from sparking curiosity to producing something uniquely meaningful, works toward the ultimate goal: engaging students in deep, authentic learning. It avoids the pitfalls of busywork and transforms the creative challenge into a deliberate, scaffolded process.

Small actions lead to big consequences. The way I chose to interpret that was by making the water that the clock is dripping into have a ripple effect. The ripple effect represents the fact that whatever you do will create a ripple effect or butterfly effect, meaning a small action can cause a bigger impact. I used a vintage clock with a crack through it to show how you can successfully go back in time, a butterfly coming from it (butterfly effect), a clock dripping into the water which creates a ripple effect, and small symbols from the butterfly effect movie. (mailbox, alcohol glass, Evans notebook, and doors). I tried to make the clock a spiral to show that time travel is sort of never ending and uncontrollable. I tried to transform that topic by making the small actions (little white pictures), small compared to the clock and everything else in the picture; the clock is melting into the water, making the "small actions" or the little drawings, melt into the "big consequences," or the water's ripple effect. These connect to the topic of small actions lead to big consequences because those small (or somewhat small) actions like them blowing up the mailbox, Tommy and Kayleigh being abused, and Evan's blackouts and actions as a kid all lead to really drastic results later in the movie. I didn't take many creative risks for this project, but I did use clay because I got the idea of using mixed media from ChatGPT and decided to use it. I wanted to use clay to make the ripple effect stand out to put more emphasis on it.

FIGURE 3.2 Student Art and Reflection for *The Butterfly Effect*

The Framework

The framework consists of five interconnected stages designed to guide students through meaningful and engaging learning experiences:

1. **Engaging Input:** Begin with rich, thought-provoking content or experiences that spark curiosity and establish a context for learning.
2. **Process Filters:** Encourage students to engage deeply with the material by analyzing, organizing, and personalizing their understanding through scaffolded tasks.
3. **Creative Output:** Challenge students to synthesize their learning into unique, original products that reflect creativity, analysis, and critical thinking.
4. **Reflection:** Provide opportunities for students to examine their processes, choices, and growth, connecting their work to broader themes and personal insights.

5. **AI Integration:** Integrate AI into one or more stages, using it as a supportive tool to enhance rather than replace students' efforts and creativity.

This framework ensures that each stage builds on the last, transforming traditional learning into a dynamic process that prioritizes creativity, critical thinking, and authentic engagement. These stages tend to work sequentially except for stage #5: AI Integration. This one is a wild card that gets fitted into one or more of the other stages as needed/suggested/demanded by the lesson. More details on that are given after discussion of stages 1 through 4.

Engaging Input

Start every unit with rich, engaging content (e.g., literature, multimedia, or introduction to a concept) that establishes context and provokes curiosity. Exactly what the engaging input is depends on the unit, your students, your approach as a teacher, and your imagination. It can be a film or a book, but it doesn't have to be. In fact, frontloading an entire text or "block" of content may not be as engaging as teasing students with a question or problem.

One educator from whom you can learn about fostering engagement is Ramsay Musallam. In his TED Talk and his book *Spark Learning*, he describes the "sweet spot" of giving students "just enough information … to create maximum curiosity" (Musallam 16). Withholding key details about something, Musallam tells us, creates an intellectual vacuum that can only be satisfied with information.

Similarly, filmmaker J. J. Abrams describes his idea of the "Mystery Box." Abrams describes how to create curiosity and engagement by creating a story with multiple mysteries. Mystery, according to Abrams, sparks imagination and curiosity that keeps the audience wanting more (TED). Essayist Derek Lieu points out that although Abrams's style of storytelling has its critics, the mystery box is perfect for movie trailers (Lieu). The goal of a successful movie trailer, says Lieu, "is to show the effects of the mysterious thing, but hide the cause. Therefore, planting the question 'What is the thing which could cause all of this!?' Instant mystery box!"

Engaging Input Examples

Input	Description	Examples
Short Videos	Use brief, high-quality videos that introduce key themes or concepts in an engaging way.	Use a documentary clip on the causes of World War I (WWI), ending right before the outbreak to spark curiosity.
Mystery-Based Prompts	Withhold key information and encourage students to explore or hypothesize based on clues.	Provide only the outcome of an equation and ask students to determine how it was solved.
Thought-Provoking Questions	Pose open-ended questions that require students to think deeply and make connections.	*"What might cause a community to turn against its own members?"*
Engaging Visuals	Use powerful or intriguing images to generate curiosity and discussion.	Display a colorful electron microscope image of a cell and have students guess its function.
Fictionalized News or Artifacts	Create fake news articles, diary entries, or artifacts for students to analyze.	Present a "found" diary entry from a soldier in the trenches of WWI.
Case Studies	Introduce a real or fictional scenario that ties directly into the topic of study.	Use a medical case study involving symptoms for students to diagnose.
Interactive Simulations	Use digital tools or role-playing to immerse students in the content.	Create a mock witch trial where students take on roles and debate evidence.
Puzzles or Riddles	Frame content as a challenge to be solved.	Give students a puzzle where the answer leads to the next equation.
Personal Reflection Prompts	Tie content to students' lives or emotions to create a personal connection.	"If you could change one law in history, what would it be and why?"
Dramatic Contrasts	Show two contrasting perspectives or outcomes to provoke discussion.	Show maps before and after a major war, asking students to infer the changes.

Process Filters

This is where the "getting down to business" work happens. It's where the student begins the journey of finding out what the thing that's causing all of this is. Process filters ensure that students engage with and organize knowledge, fostering understanding before synthesizing it into a product. Process filters contribute to student learning in a deliberate, scaffolded way that allow students to start answering questions created by the Engaging Input

Process filter tasks like note-taking and evidence-gathering act as filters and require active student involvement that prevents simple regurgitation of content or AI outputs. The filter is a way for students to get the important stuff from raw information. Filters emphasize personalization (e.g., students must reframe or reinterpret content in their own words) and collaboration (e.g., teams work together on prioritizing what's important).

Process Filter Examples

Process	Description	Example
Evidence Analysis	Students engage critically with sources to identify patterns, themes, or relevant data.	Compare two primary sources about the causes of the Civil War, noting differences in perspective.
Guided Note-Taking	Students complete structured worksheets or graphic organizers to organize their thoughts.	Fill out a T-chart comparing the motivations of two characters in a novel.
Question Generation	Students create their own questions about the material to guide discussion or further research.	Create discussion questions about the impact of deforestation on biodiversity.
Collaborative Brainstorming	Students work in groups to share ideas and organize them into a cohesive format.	Develop a list of culinary menu options that reflect seasonal ingredients.
Source Evaluation	Students critique the credibility, bias, or relevance of a source.	Analyze the reliability of a study on the effects of sugar on heart health.

(Continued)

Process	Description	Example
Evidence Collection	Students collect evidence or data that will later be used in their final product.	Record observations from a photosynthesis experiment.
Data Visualization	Students create charts, graphs, or visual organizers to represent data or concepts.	Graph a system of equations to find the point of intersection.
Prototype or Draft Creation	Students create an initial version of their final product for feedback and revision.	Build a cardboard prototype of a bridge design.
Peer Review Preparation	Students prepare materials for peer feedback, such as annotated drafts or outlines.	Highlight sections in an essay draft where feedback is needed.
Reflective Question Prompts	Students answer targeted questions to clarify their understanding before moving forward.	"What are the long-term effects of the Industrial Revolution evident in today's economy?"
Observation and Recording	Students observe phenomena or processes and record detailed notes.	Record the behaviors of fruit flies in different environmental conditions.
Concept Mapping	Students use concept maps to visualize relationships between ideas or events.	Design a concept map showing relationships between elements in the periodic table.

A process filter is a way for students to engage deeply, personalize their learning, and collaborate meaningfully.

Creative Output

The creative output is a tangible product requiring creativity and analysis and/or synthesis (e.g., essays, videos, artworks, posters, presentations), which culminate learning in an original product that cannot easily be outsourced to AI. Creative outputs are multimodal, allowing for diverse student strengths while showcasing original thinking.

The purpose of the creative output is for students to use information/evidence "captured" in the process filter to inform an original expression of that information. A creative output assignment is the perfect place to differentiate by offering a variety of options (suggestions) for accomplishing analysis and synthesis of the process filter information. A creative output assignment can look something like this:

> Now that you've gathered evidence statements from *The Crucible* about the topic you chose, use these insights to create a product that analyzes your topic using ideas from *How to Read Literature Like a Professor (HTRLLAP)*. Your product should reflect the themes, events, and analysis you've explored in your note sheet in a visual—even abstract—way. Choose one of the provided options or propose your own idea that best showcases your topic and chosen *HTRLLAP* chapter.

Product Choice	*Description*
Puritan Newspaper Article	Write a historical newspaper article as if you're reporting on events in Salem during the witch trials. Include evidence tied to your chosen *HTRLLAP* chapter.
Character Radio Broadcast	Script and record a radio broadcast from the perspective of one of the characters to reflect analysis from your chosen *HTRLLAP* chapter.
Symbolic Artwork or Collage	Create a painting, drawing, or collage symbolizing a key theme from *The Crucible*. Include a brief explanation of the connection to *HTRLLAP* analysis.
Character Diary Entries	Write a series of diary entries from a character's perspective, chronicling their thoughts during the witch trials and reflecting analysis from your *HTRLLAP* chapter.
Public Service Announcement (PSA)	Design a PSA for modern audiences based on themes from *The Crucible*. It can be an audio or video, highlighting analysis from *HTRLLAP*.
Scene Diorama	Create a diorama of a significant scene from *The Crucible*, incorporating symbols and imagery that reflect your *HTRLLAP* analysis.

(Continued)

Product Choice	Description
Thematic Timeline	Construct a timeline of *The Crucible*'s events, focusing on the development of your *HTRLLAP* topic with annotated entries.
Movie Poster	Design a movie poster for an adaptation of *The Crucible*, visually reflecting your *HTRLLAP* topic with imagery, colors, and taglines.
Abstract Poetry or Visual Poem	Create a visual or abstract poem representing *The Crucible*'s emotional journey to express your *HTRLLAP* analysis.
Historical Exhibit Poster	Make a poster for an imaginary museum exhibit on *The Crucible*, curating artifacts with labels connecting them to your *HTRLLAP* topic.
Your Own Idea	Propose your own creative idea to the teacher, ensuring it represents your *HTRLLAP* topic and reflects your understanding of *The Crucible*.

The rubric for this assignment spells out expectations without binding them to physical and structural criteria that kill creativity:

Criteria	*Wanting (One Point)*	*Worthy (Three Points)*	*Exemplary (Five Points)*
Creativity	Little originality or creativity, lacks uniqueness and innovation.	Some originality and creativity. Demonstrates some uniqueness and innovation.	Demonstrates strong originality and creativity, with a unique and innovative approach.
Understanding	Demonstrates minimal understanding; lacks connection to themes/messages.	Partial understanding/somewhat clear connection to themes/messages.	Shows a solid understanding, with a clear and insightful connection.
Execution	Inaccurate representation or weak connection to the chosen *HTRLLAP* topic.	Partially represents and explores the *HTRLLAP* topic in *The Crucible*.	Accurately represents and explores the *HTRLLAP* topic in *The Crucible*.
Relevance	Not relevant/lacks connection to the central themes of *The Crucible*.	Partially relevant/partially connects with the central themes of *The Crucible*.	Highly relevant/effectively connects with the central themes of *The Crucible*.

(Continued)

Criteria	Wanting (One Point)	Worthy (Three Points)	Exemplary (Five Points)
Integration of *HTRLLAP* Concepts	*HTRLLAP* concepts are not effectively integrated; lacks cohesion.	Partial integration of *HTRLLAP* concepts; has some cohesion.	Effectively integrates *HTRLLAP* concepts, demonstrating cohesion.

The unique and creative nature of a creative output product discourages having AI do the assignment, relegating it at most to an advisory role. This is where students can develop a sense of pride in what they create. And because of that, allow creative output assignment prompts to be vague as opposed to formulatory. Keep specifications and rubrics simple so that there is room for innovation and creativity.

The above rubric is open-ended enough to include any of the listed products. And the rubric intentionally does not quantify (like number of words, pages, slides, minutes, etc.). Students will actually stretch to fill that vagueness with quality instead of worrying about meeting some arbitrary quantity criteria.

What if a student doesn't? What if they take advantage of the vagueness? Give them time. When the culture of the class is one of creative quality, they will come around because they don't want to miss out on the fun.

One of the key features of the creative output is the showcase. Unlike a traditional presentation (reading word-for-word from a series of PowerPoint slides), the showcase is more like something at an art gallery. Students are the unique experts about an original product that they created, and that expertise translates into enthusiasm. It's hard to be enthusiastic about content that you copy/paste from Wikipedia; but it's next to impossible to not be enthusiastic about an original piece of art, for example, that incorporates analysis and synthesis from the source material in an original style from a unique perspective. And when everyone else in the class has had a shared experience with the source material, a creative interpretation of that source material is energizing and engaging.

A rubric such as the following one covers speaking/presenting skills for just about any presentation:

Criteria	Wanting (One Point)	Worthy (Three Points)	Exemplary (Five Points)
Delivery	You were unclear and difficult to hear, with poor eye contact and body language. You looked at the teacher a lot.	You were somewhat clear and audible, with occasional eye contact and acceptable body language. You looked at the teacher too much.	You were clear and audible, maintaining good eye contact and appropriate body language throughout the presentation. You looked at the audience, not the teacher.
Organization	Presentation lacked structure, making it hard to follow, with no clear introduction, body, or conclusion.	Presentation had some structure but may have been confusing at times, with an attempt at an introduction, body, and conclusion.	Presentation was well-structured and easy to follow, with a clear introduction, body, and conclusion.

The showcase has a built in audience, and it can be given authenticity with interactive engagement. "Interactive" is a key concept here. When the audience is a captive one (like our students), true engagement can be difficult. Giving the audience something to do—making them an active participant—can make a huge difference. Not only do the students find themselves learning from their classmates, but students develop a greater sense of purpose when presenting in such an environment.

There are different ways to attain interactive engagement. Students can include an interactive element with their showcase in the form of checks for understanding (Quizlet, Kahoot, Google Form, etc.). Or you can convert the product and presentation rubrics into evaluation questions on a Google Form. This changes the role of the student audience from passive audience member to an evaluative role. The evaluation of each other's products and presentations among students helps them internalize expectations as well as provide authentic feedback. For that reason, I include a space for feedback that students love getting the next day.

Creating questions from the product rubric and the showcase rubric provides feedback that is aligned with those rubrics.

A Google Form that students in the audience fill out during each presentation keeps them engaged and gives them a purpose. See Figure 3.3.

Reflection

The reflection is where the ultimate learning magic happens. This is where students analyze their processes and learning, including how they used tools like AI. Middle school teacher Brooke B. Eisenbach, writing for the Association for Middle Level Education, says reflection allows students to "identify their newfound knowledge and see their own growth and awareness of the content" (Eisenbach). In other words, intentional content-based reflection allows students to make sense and internalize what they are learning:

> It is through reflection that students make individual and collective meaning of their experiences, connect those experiences to past and future learning, and build new neural networks. Learners need time and structures to process their experiences, just as our bodies need time to digest food and transform it into usable nutrients.
>
> (Buck Institute for Education)

Reflection assignments differ from traditional essays in both length and purpose. An academic essay is meant to present a clear argument on a specific topic with evidence from reliable sources. A reflection is a personal type of writing where a student

Rate your classmate's "The Crucible PRODUCT SHOWCASE" from 1 (not really very good) to 3 (really good!).

	1	2	3
How creative and original is the product?	○	○	○
How well does the product show that they understood the themes and messages?	○	○	○
How well does the product connect with the HTRLLAP topic?	○	○	○
How well does the product relate to the main themes of "The Crucible"?	○	○	○
How well are the HTRLLAP concepts included and explained by the product?	○	○	○
Does the presenter speak clearly and look at the audience?	○	○	○
Is the presentation structured with a clear beginning, middle, and end?	○	○	○

Please leave positive, constructive feedback.

Your answer

FIGURE 3.3 Peer Review Form Screenshot

explores their own experiences and feelings about a topic. The following prompt provides enough guidance so the student can make a suitable reflection without having to specify things like length.

> Reflect on your experiences and learning from this AI unit. In your reflection, consider how the skills and knowledge you gained about AI apply to different aspects of your life, both inside and outside of school. Use specific examples. Consider the following questions to guide your reflection:
>
> ♦ How has learning about AI tools and their applications changed the way you approach your schoolwork and how do you plan to use AI to improve your studies in the future?
> ♦ How do you think the understanding and experience with AI you gained in this unit might benefit you in your future career?

Student reflections are varied yet relevant.

> Learning about AI tools changed how I do my schoolwork and the quality of my work before sending it in. Before learning about AI tools, I spent most of the time I was given for an assignment brainstorming. For example, I used AI to suggest different scripts and formats when I had to write a script for my AI collaborative writing newscast project. If I did not know how to utilize AI for brainstorming, I would've wasted more time that could've been used for my project. In my other classes, like Math, AI is helpful when my teacher's explanation is not sufficient to get through a packet, and it can break down what I am doing into as many smaller, more straightforward steps as I want. AI is great for schoolwork in the present but I also wouldn't want to become too reliant on it.

> In this unit, I learned to be better with my AI prompting and to continue adding to a prompt until I get what I want. I think that learning persistence and continuing to evolve a prompt/answer are good life skills, such as when I sew and have to keep altering my product until it fits. In school, it's good to keep trying on assignments and, if possible, resubmit until you get the right answer. I don't think AI influences my schoolwork, and I don't plan to use it. In most cases, I think it's more stress and work than doing things by hand. I find the foundation of AI's answers are often flimsy. I think that in the future, I want to be a teacher, and AI could be used to create practice prompts/problems.

AI Integration

When students are trained how to prompt AI, it can be positioned as a supportive, scaffolding tool rather than a replacement, emphasizing critical thinking and human oversight. In other words, tasks are designed so AI augments the process (e.g., generating topics or organizing ideas) while requiring students to refine or apply the outputs creatively.

With that in mind, you can include AI as part of an assignment. Including it as a part of the assignment intentionally excludes AI such as ChatGPT as an agent of cheating. The following tables have examples of AI as a supportive/scaffolding tool categorized by the first three stages of the five-stage framework: engaging input, process filters, and creative output. Each task includes example prompts.

Engaging Input
Use AI to lower barriers to entry for topics, ensuring students feel curious before diving into content.

Goal: to spark curiosity and provide context for learning

Task	Description	Example Prompt
Topic Exploration	Students brainstorm broad topics or research questions, using ChatGPT to expand their ideas.	"I'm brainstorming ideas for a project on teen mental health. Can you suggest key issues related to these topics?"
Vocabulary Support	Students upload terms they need to understand, and ChatGPT generates definitions, explanations, and examples.	"I need help in understanding terms related to cellular respiration. Can you provide definitions and examples?"
Representation Ideas	Students brainstorm creative ways to represent learning visually or artistically.	"I'm researching the Industrial Revolution. Can you suggest creative ways to present my findings, like multimedia or artistic formats?"

Process Filters

Encourage active learning by requiring students to process their own notes or collected data.

Goal: to ensure students interact deeply with the material

Task	Description	Example Prompt
Organizing Student Notes	Students upload notes or research, and ChatGPT organizes them into meaningful categories or themes.	"Can you organize my notes on the Civil Rights Movement into social, political, and economic impacts?"
Visualizing Topics	Students provide notes or topics, and ChatGPT narrows them down and suggests a graphic organizer.	"Here are my topics from *Born a Crime*. Can you help narrow these down to two and suggest a graphic organizer to map connections?"
Analyzing Patterns	Students upload quotes, evidence, or data for ChatGPT to identify patterns or connections.	"What themes connect these quotes about biodiversity and deforestation? Can you summarize them?"
Structuring Notes	Students upload notes, and ChatGPT synthesizes them into a study guide.	"Can you organize my notes on World War II into a clear, concise study guide?"

(Continued)

Task	Description	Example Prompt
Data Trend Analysis	Students upload data (e.g., spreadsheets or survey results) for ChatGPT to identify trends or anomalies.	"Here's my spreadsheet on plant growth under different light conditions. Can you identify trends or patterns in the data?"

Creative Output

Focus on guiding students in structuring and presenting their work without replacing the original thinking process.

Goal: to guide students in producing meaningful, original outputs

Task	Description	Example Prompt
Outlining Steps for a Task	Students use ChatGPT to create step-by-step plans for completing assignments.	"I'm preparing a three-course meal. Can you help me create a checklist for preparing and plating each dish?"
Script Drafting	Students upload research or outlines, and ChatGPT helps turn them into a coherent script.	"I need help writing a script for a video presentation on the ethical considerations of gene editing based on my research notes."
Peer Feedback Simulation	Students upload drafts, and ChatGPT provides feedback to improve clarity and depth.	"Here's my storyboard for a short film. Can you provide suggestions for improvement as if you were a peer reviewer?"

Each task explicitly uses student-generated input as the starting point, emphasizing the role of AI as a tool to enhance student learning rather than replace it. This ensures that students remain active participants in their learning process.

Consideration must be given to the use of AI in a stage of the framework to the weight of the score for that stage. For example, when AI creates a script for a skit or video (creative output) based on a graphic organizer of evidence collected by the student (process filter), the graphic organizer represents a task requiring significant student input whereas the script is merely a product made with AI support. So the graphic organizer logically carries more weight than the script when assessing critical thinking and the effort that accompanies it.

When assigning points to each stage of the framework, emphasize students' effort, creativity, and critical thinking over AI-generated contributions:

- Assign higher weights to tasks requiring significant student input, such as evidence collection and creative products.
- Assign lower weights to tasks supported by AI to reinforce its role as a tool rather than a substitute for learning.

Look at the following example unit and the weight assigned to each component. In this unit, students explore the concept of the five stages of grief through Edgar Allan Poe's "The Raven." The unit begins by engaging students with an introductory video and reflection, followed by a deep dive into analyzing The Raven for evidence of the five stages. Using their findings, students create an original multimedia product, such as a song or a video, to synthesize their learning. They then present their work to the class. Finally, the unit concludes with a reflection that ties their creative work and analysis to broader themes of grief and human experience.

Engaging Input

- Assignment:
  Students begin by watching a short, curated video explaining the five stages of grief. They also complete a short reflection on how they've encountered these stages in literature, film, or personal experience.

Process Filters

- Assignment:
  Students work individually or in teams to analyze *The Raven* by Edgar Allan Poe. They identify and annotate examples of the five stages of grief in the text. This includes creating a detailed note sheet with evidence statements from the poem, organized by stage.

Creative Output

- Product Assignment:
  Using their note sheet, students create a multimedia product to represent the five stages of grief in *The Raven*. Options include:
  ◊ a poem or song
  ◊ a short video reenacting key moments in the stages
  ◊ a symbolic artwork
- AI Support:
  ChatGPT can suggest creative approaches or provide scripts, timelines, or outlines for multimedia projects.
- Showcase Assignment:
  Students present their creative products to the class in a short presentation. They explain their artistic choices, demonstrate their understanding of the five stages of grief, and respond to audience questions.

Reflection

- Assignment:
  Students write a reflection explaining how their creative product illustrates the five stages of grief and the relevance of the stages to broader human experiences.

Weighting for the Five Stages of Grief Unit

Stage	Assignment	Weight	Rationale
Engaging Input	Video viewing and short reflection	10%	Encourages curiosity and initial exploration of the five stages of grief.
Process Filters	Text analysis and note sheet creation using *The Raven*	30%	Rewards detailed and thoughtful interaction with the material.

(Continued)

Stage	Assignment	Weight	Rationale
Creative Output	Multimedia product creation	15%	Emphasizes originality and synthesis of learning, supported by AI as a tool for scaffolding creativity.
	Showcase	15%	Recognizes communication and presentation skills while sharing their learning journey.
Reflection	Analytical and creative reflection	30%	Highlights analytical and critical thinking skills in connecting evidence to themes.

Weight distribution doesn't follow a strict rule but represents a teacher's assessment of student effort, creativity, and critical thinking versus AI-generated contribution.

As we navigate an age shaped by rapid technological advancement, this framework offers more than a strategy to coexist with AI—it provides a commitment to preserving the essence of human learning. By focusing on engaging inputs, process-driven exploration, creative outputs, and reflection, educators can empower students to take ownership of their learning while skillfully integrating AI as a supportive tool.

Chapter 3 Postscript: Ethical Considerations

Teachers need to design instruction with these ethical issues in mind:

- **Data Security:** As students engage in project-based learning using AI tools, the security of their data is crucial. Ethical concerns include how student data is stored, accessed, and potentially shared. Educators need to ensure that the AI tools they use comply with data protection laws and that they educate students on the importance of data privacy (Soares; Maddux).

- **Bias in AI Algorithms:** Differentiated instruction relies on AI to tailor learning experiences based on individual student profiles. However, AI algorithms contain systematic biases based on the data it's trained on. It's essential for educators to be aware that societal biases are contained in datasets used to train AI systems. AI might recommend content or unfairly evaluate certain students, affecting grades, feedback, and academic progression ("AI Biases Explained—Learn More about Them"; "Addressing Bias in AI | Center for Teaching Excellence").
- **Environmental Impact of AI Technologies:** AI systems consume significant energy, contributing to environmental concerns. Educators should consider the environmental costs of using AI technologies and seek to use resources that commit to sustainable practices (Cho; "12 Key Principles for Sustainable AI").
- **AI and a Future Job Market:** As AI increasingly becomes a tool for crafting and supporting education, it also reshapes the job market that students will enter. This raises concerns about the skills students need to compete in an AI-driven economy. As curriculums adapt to include AI literacy, ensure that students are prepared not just to use AI but to understand and innovate with it ethically (Demirci et al.; Jenner et al.; NAESP Staff).

Works Cited

"12 Key Principles for Sustainable AI." *Access Partnership*, 5 Feb. 2025, https://accesspartnership.com/12-key-principles-for-sustainable-ai/.

"Addressing Bias in AI | Center for Teaching Excellence." Center for Teaching Excellence, The University of Kansas, 2025, https://cte.ku.edu/addressing-bias-ai.

"AI Biases Explained—Learn More about Them." *Covisian*, 24 June 2024, https://covisian.com/tech-post/ai-biases-explained-learn-more-about-them/.

"Authentic Assessment." Center for Innovative Teaching and Learning, Indiana University Bloomington, 2025, https://citl.indiana.edu/teaching-resources/assessing-student-learning/authentic-assessment/index.html.

Biggs, John. "Constructive Alignment." *John Biggs*, n.d., https://www.johnbiggs.com.au/academic/constructive-alignment/.

Cho, Renée. "AI's Growing Carbon Footprint – State of the Planet." *State of the Planet*, 9 June 2023, https://news.climate.columbia.edu/2023/06/09/ais-growing-carbon-footprint/.

Demirci, Ozge, et al. "Research: How Gen AI Is Already Impacting the Labor Market." *Harvard Business Review*, 11 Nov. 2024, https://hbr.org/2024/11/research-how-gen-ai-is-already-impacting-the-labor-market.

Eisenbach, Brooke B. "Student Reflection: A Tool for Growth and Development." *AMLE*, n.d., https://www.amle.org/student-reflection-a-tool-for-growth-and-development/.

Gonzalez, Jennifer. "Is Your Lesson a Grecian Urn?" *Cult of Pedagogy*, 30 Oct. 2016, https://www.cultofpedagogy.com/grecian-urn-lesson/.

Jenner, Caroline, et al. "Teaching Students to Embrace AI Responsibly." *Edtech Digest*, 26 Feb. 2024, https://www.edtechdigest.com/2024/02/26/teaching-students-to-embrace-ai-responsibly/.

Kelly, Jack. "AI-Skilled Workers Are the New, Hot, In-Demand Professionals." *Forbes*, 1 Aug. 2024, https://www.forbes.com/sites/jackkelly/2024/08/01/ai-skilled-workers-are-the-new-hot-in-demand-professionals/.

Lieu, Derek. "J.J. Abrams' Mystery Box Was Designed for Trailers." *Derek Lieu Creative*, 10 Jan. 2020, https://www.derek-lieu.com/blog/2020/1/10/jj-abrams-mystery-box-was-designed-for-trailers.

Maddux, Christopher. "The Importance of Student Data Privacy." *Education Technology Insights*, 2025, https://stem.educationtechnologyinsights.com/cxoinsights/the-importance-of-student-data-privacy-nid-2435.html.

"Metacognition | Columbia CTL." Columbia Center for Teaching and Learning, Columbia University, 2018, https://ctl.columbia.edu/resources-and-technology/resources/metacognition/.

Musallam, Ramsey. *Spark Learning: 3 Keys to Embracing the Power of Student Curiosity*. Dave Burgess Consulting, Incorporated, 2017.

NAESP Staff. "5 Strategies for Success in Bringing AI to Schools." *NAESP*, The National Association of Elementary School Principals Foundation, 26 Aug. 2023, https://www.naesp.org/resource/5-strategies-for-success-in-bringing-ai-to-schools/.

"Reflecting with Purpose in PBL." *PBLworks*, Buck Institute for Education, 22 Feb. 2022, https://www.pblworks.org/blog/reflecting-purpose-pbl.

Soares, Wellington. "AI Platform Use by Teachers Leads to Student Privacy Worries." *Chalkbeat*, 13 Dec. 2024, https://www.chalkbeat.org/2024/12/13/ai-tools-used-by-teachers-can-put-student-privacy-and-data-at-risk/.

TED. "The Mystery Box | JJ Abrams." *YouTube*, TED, 14 Jan. 2008, https://www.youtube.com/watch?v=vpjVgF5JDq8.

Tomlinson, Carol Ann. "What Is Differentiated Instruction?" Reading Rockets, WETA, 2025, https://www.readingrockets.org/topics/differentiated-instruction/articles/what-differentiated-instruction.

"What Is Experiential Learning?" Institute for Experiential Learning, 2025, https://experientiallearninginstitute.org/what-is-experiential-learning/.

"What Is Project Based Learning?" PBLWorks, Buck Institute for Education, n.d., https://www.pblworks.org/what-is-pbl.

4
Unit Structures for AI-Integrated Learning

Here are the foundations for the pedagogical practices discussed in this chapter:

Constructivism (by Dewey; Piaget; Bruner): It emphasizes active learning where students build knowledge through experiences ("Constructivism in Education"). The chapter's use of various structures, such as branching pathways and cycles, aligns with constructivist ideas, allowing students to interact with content in diverse ways that enhance understanding.

Universal Design for Learning: It advocates for providing multiple means of engagement, representation, action, and expression ("Universal Design for Learning | Accessibility Resources at UNCG"). The branching pathways and hybrid models introduced in this chapter provide different avenues for learning, which is a core principle of UDL, catering to varied learning needs and preferences.

Bloom's Taxonomy (by Bloom): It organizes educational goals into cognitive levels of complexity and specificity (Stapleton-Corcoran). The framework's stages from engaging input to creative output and reflection can be seen as moving higher-order skills (apply, analyze, create).

Differentiation: It focuses on adjusting the teaching strategies, materials, and assessments to accommodate the diverse needs of learners (Tomlinson). The chapter's discussion of providing different pathways and adjusting project requirements based on student needs reflects this theory.

Formative Assessment: It involves assessments designed to gather feedback to improve and accelerate learning (Laitusis). The cycle model, with its emphasis on iteration and continuous feedback, aligns with formative assessment practices.

Metacognition: It involves students' awareness of their own knowledge and their ability to understand, control, and manipulate their own cognitive processes (Sword). The reflection stage in each unit encourages metacognitive skills by asking students to think about their learning process and outcomes.

Chapter 3 described units using the framework in a linear way. In other words, the sequence goes from engaging input, the process filter, creative output, and then reflection. Of course, it makes sense for units to start with something engaging and end with reflection, but there is room for mixing it up in between.

Once you get comfortable with the five-stage framework, you can start to get creative with putting the pieces together in different ways.

Take, for example, another unit on the five stages of grief. After an engaging introductory video, students analyze the song

"Bohemian Rhapsody," collecting evidence of the five stages in the song using a supplied graphic organizer. Students then create a multimedia product, such as a painting or video, that represents Freddie Mercury's journey through the five stages. They then showcase their work to the class. The unit concludes with a written reflection that ties their creative work to broader themes of grief and human experience.

This unit can be represented visually in a linear fashion, as shown in Figure 4.1.

The learning emphasis for this kind of activity is the collection of evidence (process filter) and the written analysis of the creative output (reflection). The creative output provides a medium for the reflection. Thus, it may be helpful for the student to enlist some help from ChatGPT for the creative output. The

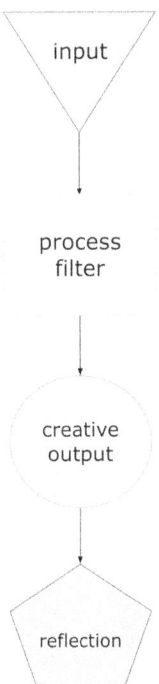

FIGURE 4.1 Linear Model

student can "dump" their notes into ChatGPT along with a prompt like this:

> I've uploaded my graphic organizer with evidence of the five stages of grief from Bohemian Rhapsody. Can you suggest creative ideas for an artistic representation of Freddie Mercury's journey through these stages? I'm thinking of a product like a painting that captures the emotions and themes from my notes.

The unit is still linear only with an artificial intelligence (AI) component added, as shown in Figure 4.2.

But some of my students might prefer to produce a more "conventional" product in the form of an essay. Why hold them to making something visually creative when their creative passion is writing essays? This is where you can add another

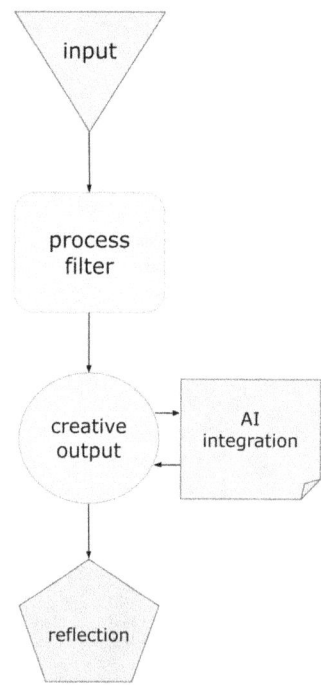

FIGURE 4.2 Linear Model with AI Integration

pathway: write an essay and then explain it to the class for the showcase. Since the product—whether a piece of art or an essay—is not the learning emphasis, each creative output path is just a way to get from the process filter to the reflection. Now the unit is no longer linear, as shown in Figure 4.3.

It is now a unit model with branching pathways. And AI integration for the essay path can be an AI-created outline from the graphic organizer. The input is the student's—ChatGPT is just helping to organize it.

This branching pathways model is really just a choice menu that teachers often offer their students. Framing it this way reveals where the student learning actually takes place (process filter and reflection) and where the activity is an expression or interpretation

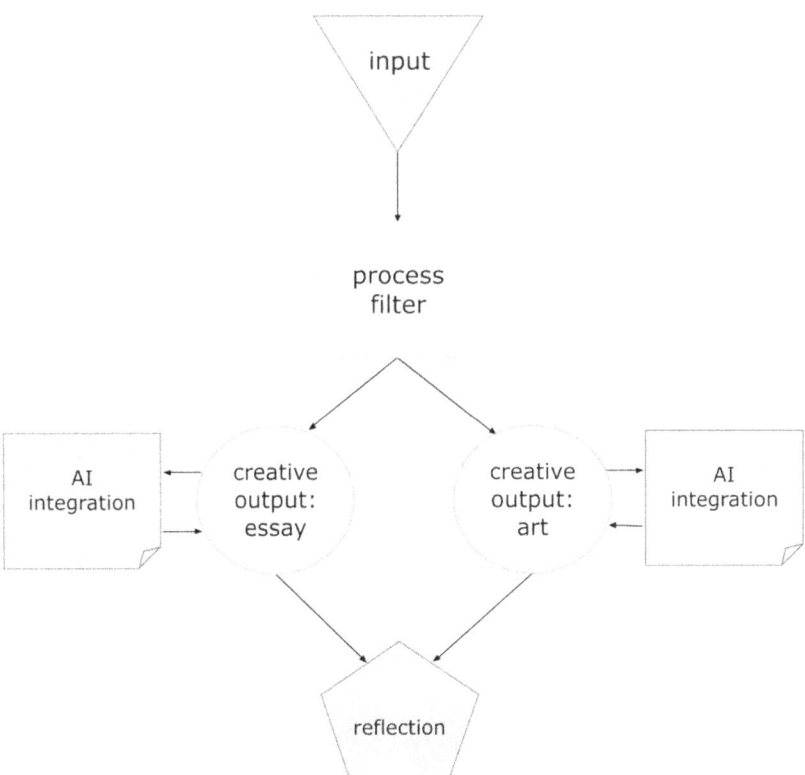

FIGURE 4.3 Branching Pathways Model

of that learning (creative output). Framing it in these terms also makes it easier to justify weighting stages differently.

What if the purpose of the unit is actually writing essays? You can make the essay writing process a learning objective rather than an option by putting the unit back into the linear form and adding a series of peer edits—first AI, then student peer edits. This addition creates a cycle model, as shown in Figure 4.4.

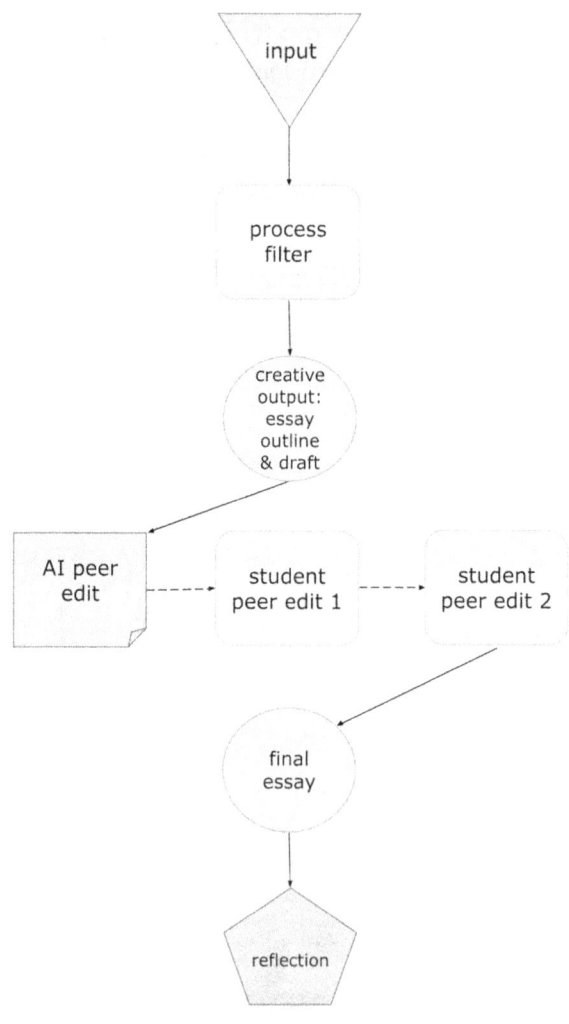

FIGURE 4.4 Essay Writing Process with Peer Edits

The cycle model encourages continuous improvement, typical in STEM and design-based projects. Students iterate on their original work, applying feedback and demonstrating growth.

But I do have some students who struggle with the essay-writing process. They can get the evidence they need on the graphic organizer, but struggle with outlining or writing the essay itself. This is where scaffolding and differentiation come in. I can provide different pathways through the original outline/draft process that provide support. Adding branching pathways does just that, as shown in Figure 4.5.

This Hybrid model is a combination of linear, branching pathways, and cycle models. Teachers can assign the outline/draft branch that suits each student and end up with a similar product output for the peer editing stage. Assign the AI outline/student draft path to students who struggle with organization so that organizing is modeled for them and reinforced when they write the draft. Assign the student outline/AI draft path to students who need to work on translating their ideas into coherent and fluid text so that they can see how it's done when written out. Students who are pretty good at both can take the middle path to hone their writing chops.

Although these examples are for a Language Arts class, the models work for all subject areas—even technical ones, especially technical ones.

For example, take an algebra unit about the quadratic equation. After an engaging video about quadratic equations and the quadratic formula, students explore multiple pathways to deepen their understanding of solving quadratics, including using the formula and alternative methods such as factoring or completing the square. The branching pathways model provides flexibility for students to engage in the method, while also comparing the strengths and limitations of each approach. AI tools are integrated to prepare a product that they then showcase. Finally, students write a short response analyzing their chosen

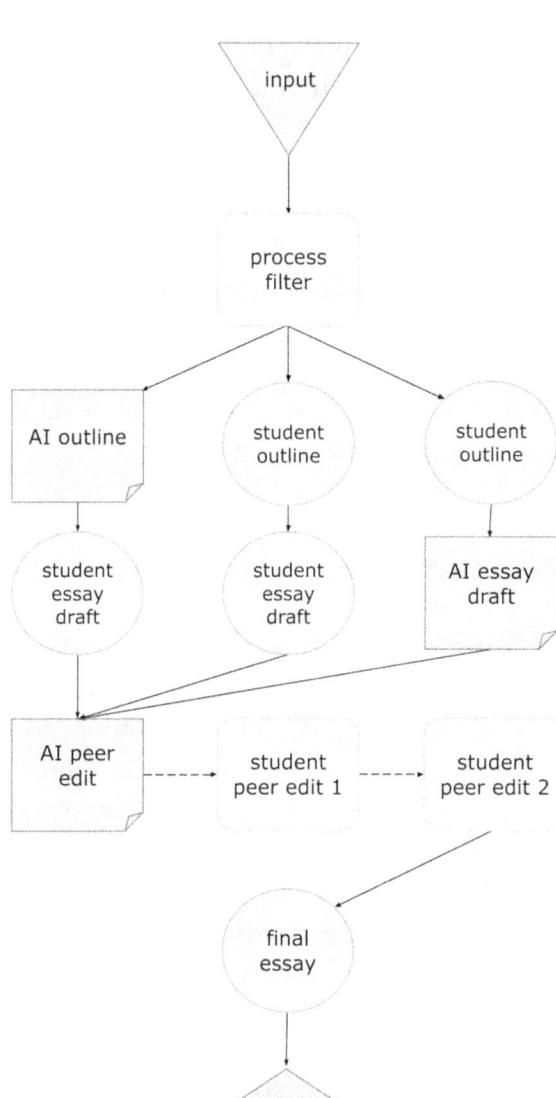

FIGURE 4.5 Essay Writing with Multiple AI Pathways

pathway, discussing its strengths, weaknesses, and their learning experience. See Figure 4.6.

Another example of a technical unit is where engineering students are tasked with exploring the principles of structural

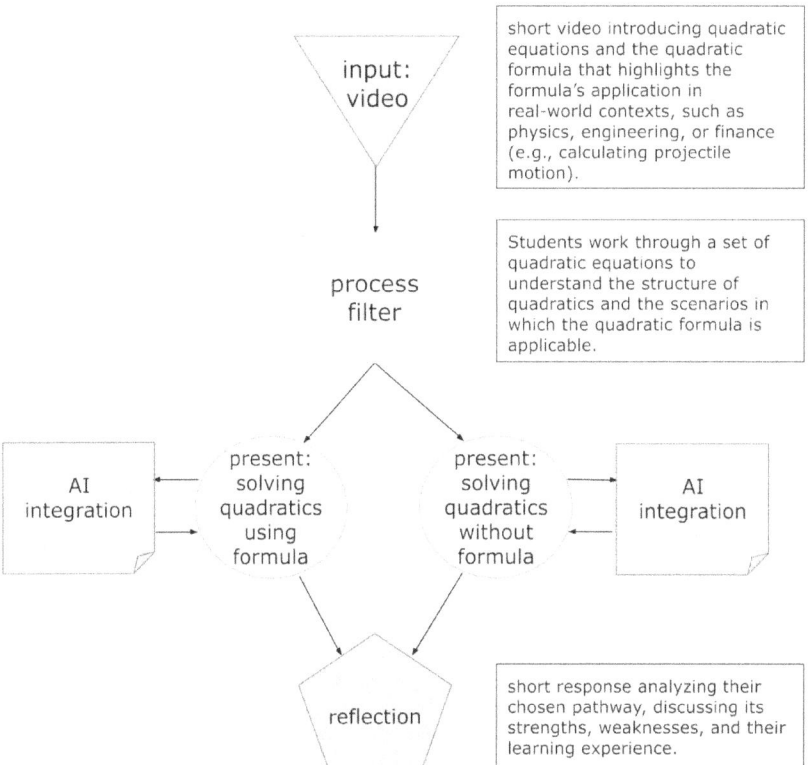

FIGURE 4.6 Quadratic Equations Pathways Model

engineering by analyzing real-world case studies of bridge successes and failures. Working in small groups, students examine challenges, solutions, and design principles from specific engineering cases and apply their findings to design and build a bridge prototype. Teams choose between two pathways: using AI to simulate stress tests and optimize their design or performing manual calculations and testing. After initial testing, teams analyze the performance of their prototypes, identify weaknesses, and refine their designs through an iterative process. The unit concludes with a showcase, where teams present their improved prototypes, engage in peer evaluations, and finally, reflect on their design choices to deepen their understanding of engineering practices. See Figure 4.7.

68 ◆ Designing Lessons in the AI-Infused Classroom

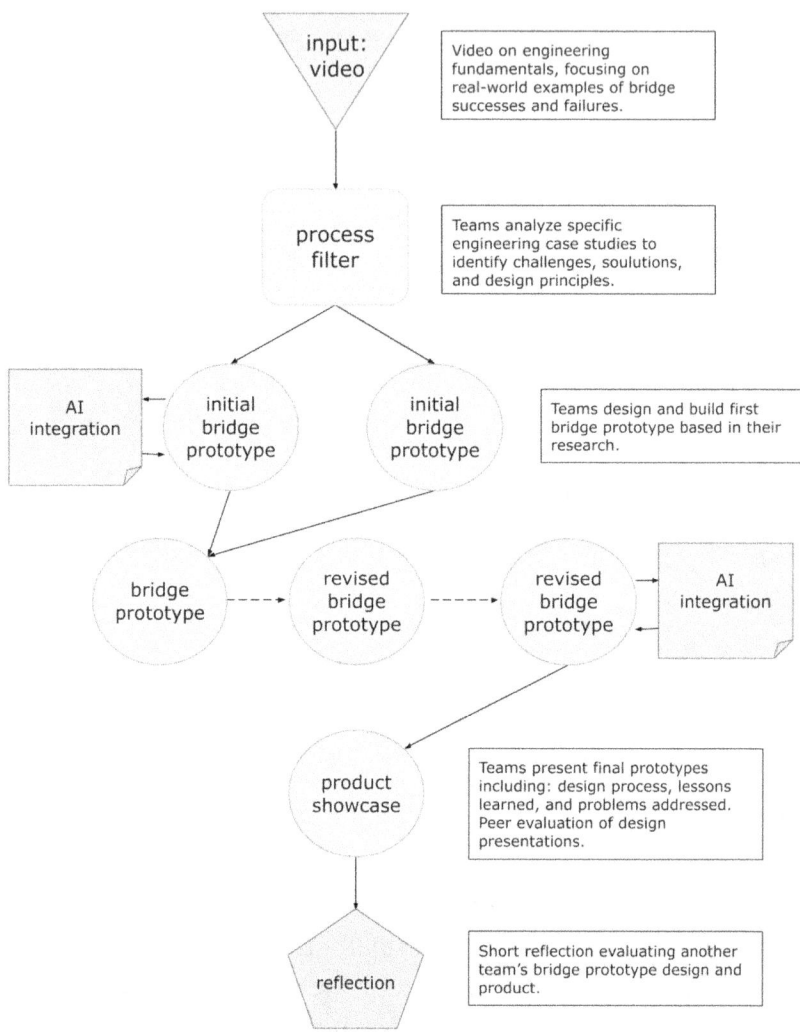

FIGURE 4.7 Bridge Engineering Project Model

To review, the four unit structure models are as follows:

Linear Model

1. **Inputs:**
   ◊ Core materials (e.g., videos, texts, multimedia content, frameworks).

◊ Designed to provide background knowledge and thematic context.
2. **Process Filter:**
   ◊ Individual tasks requiring active engagement (e.g., guided note-taking, summarizing key ideas, answering prompts).
   ◊ Collaborative activities where students work in teams to analyze, brainstorm, or synthesize information.
3. **Creative Output:**
   ◊ Students produce a final product (e.g., essays, posters, dioramas) to showcase understanding and creativity.
4. **Reflection:**
   ◊ Students evaluate their process and learning (e.g., written reflections, peer reviews, class presentations).

Branching Pathways Model

1. **Inputs:**
   ◊ Shared resources that lay the groundwork for all students (e.g., background texts, videos, or lectures).
2. **Path 1:**
   ◊ A pathway where students engage manually, emphasizing critical thinking (e.g., creating an outline or analysis from scratch).
3. **Path 2:**
   ◊ A pathway where students use AI tools to assist in their process (e.g., AI-generated outlines, brainstorming prompts).
4. **Creative Output:**
   ◊ Both pathways converge in a final creative product that demonstrates learning (e.g., a presentation, multimedia project, or essay).
5. **Reflection:**
   ◊ Students analyze their chosen approach (manual vs. AI-assisted), discuss challenges, and evaluate outcomes.

Cycle Model

1. **Inputs:**
   ◊ Introduction to key concepts and tools (e.g., theoretical frameworks, examples, or skill demonstrations).
2. **Create:**
   ◊ Students produce an initial draft, prototype, or product (e.g., a project outline, design, or rough draft).
3. **Test/Present:**
   ◊ Students share their work-in-progress through class presentations or peer reviews.
4. **Revise/Create Again:**
   ◊ Students iterate on their original work, applying feedback and demonstrating growth.
5. **Reflect:**
   ◊ Feedback and self-assessment help students refine their understanding and skills.

Hybrid Model

Structure:

1. **Inputs:**
   ◊ Core materials to introduce content and establish shared understanding (e.g., theoretical frameworks, videos, case studies).
2. **Parallel Process Filters:**
   ◊ Teams tackle one aspect of the content collaboratively (e.g., creating slides on a specific concept).
   ◊ Individuals analyze another aspect independently (e.g., completing a guided note sheet).
3. **Creative Outputs:**
   ◊ Collaborative and individual work combine in a unified product (e.g., a class presentation, thematic project, or portfolio).

4. **Revise/Create Again:**
   ◊ Students iterate on their original work, applying feedback and demonstrating growth.
5. **Reflection:**
   ◊ Students evaluate their contribution to the team and the individual work process.

There are advantages to using these models; thinking in terms of the five-stage framework: engaging input, process filters, creative output, reflection, and AI integration and arranging these stages into a unit structure model can help you and your students to focus on the learning objectives and what part of the process facilitates that learning in the AI-infused classroom. The distinctive characteristics of this framework and unit models are:

♦ **Clarity:** These models provide a clear flow for lesson/unit design.
♦ **Flexibility:** They adapt to diverse subjects and disciplines.
♦ **Student-Centered:** They emphasize creativity, accountability, and engagement.
♦ **AI Integration:** They encourage meaningful use of AI as a tool, not a replacement for learning.

The next chapter talks about (1) how to structure units based on your knowledge of your students and your goals for them and (2) when and where to include AI integration in each unit.

Chapter 4 Postscript: Ethical Considerations

Teachers need to design learning activities with these issues in mind:

♦ **Access Issues:** AI can sometimes exacerbate access issues if not all students have equal access to the technology or if the AI is not designed with all user needs in mind. Educators need

to ensure that AI tools are accessible to all students, including those with disabilities, and that these tools are capable of supporting a variety of learning requirements and needs (Devon; Stravopodis).
- **Learning Autonomy:** There is a risk that over-reliance on AI could undermine students' ability to think independently and creatively. Educators should use AI as a supportive tool that enhances student learning without replacing the need for critical thinking and problem-solving skills. It's important to strike a balance where AI assists rather than replaces the learning process (Habib; Nufer).
- **AI Adaptability:** AI systems need to learn and adapt to new educational methodologies and student interactions. There must be ongoing efforts to update and refine AI systems used in educational settings to keep pace with educational research and pedagogical practices, ensuring they remain effective and relevant (Giannini; Yin).

Works Cited

"Constructivism in Education." *UBC Master of Educational Technology Program*, 2015, https://constructivism512.weebly.com/meet-the-theorists.html.

Devon, Joe. "The Impact of AI in Advancing Accessibility for Learners with Disabilities." *EDUCAUSE Review*, 10 Sept. 2024, https://er.educause.edu/articles/2024/9/the-impact-of-ai-in-advancing-accessibility-for-learners-with-disabilities.

Giannini, Stefania. "Use of AI in Education: Deciding on the Future We Want." *UNESCO*, 16 May 2024, https://www.unesco.org/en/articles/use-ai-education-deciding-future-we-want.

Habib, Sabrina. "AI Can Help—and Hurt—Student Creativity." *University of South Carolina*, 5 Feb. 2024, https://sc.edu/uofsc/posts/2024/02/conversation-ai-help.php.

Laitusis, Vytas. "What Is the Purpose of Formative Assessment? A Look at the Process of Monitoring Student Growth." *HMH*, 21 Aug. 2023, https://www.hmhco.com/blog/what-is-the-purpose-of-formative-assessment.

Nufer, Sean. "Balancing Human Touch with AI in Education." *Canvas Community*, 21 Dec. 2023, https://community.canvaslms.com/t5/Artificial-Intelligence-in/Balancing-Human-Touch-with-AI-in-Education/ba-p/590952.

Stapleton-Corcoran, Erin. "Bloom's Taxonomy of Educational Objectives | Center for the Advancement of Teaching Excellence | University of Illinois Chicago." Center for the Advancement of Teaching Excellence, The Board of Trustees of the University of Illinois, 25 Jan. 2023, https://teaching.uic.edu/cate-teaching-guides/syllabus-course-design/blooms-taxonomy-of-educational-objectives/.

Stravopodis, Minas. "AI and Access to Education: Bridging the Digital Divide." *IRIS Sustainable Development*, 7 Mar. 2024, https://www.irissd.org/post/ai-and-access-to-education-bridging-the-digital-divide.

Sword, Rosalyn. "Metacognition | Teaching Strategies & Classroom Activities." *High Speed Training*, 17 Mar. 2021, https://www.highspeedtraining.co.uk/hub/metacognition-in-the-classroom/.

Tomlinson, Carol Ann. "What Is Differentiated Instruction?" Reading Rockets, WETA, 2025, https://www.readingrockets.org/topics/differentiated-instruction/articles/what-differentiated-instruction.

"Universal Design for Learning" Accessibility Resources at UNCG, 2025, https://accessibility.uncg.edu/for-all/udl/.

Yin, William J. "Will Our Educational System Keep Pace with AI? A Student's Perspective on AI and Learning." *EDUCAUSE Review*, 24 Jan. 2024, https://er.educause.edu/articles/2024/1/will-our-educational-system-keep-pace-with-ai-a-students-perspective-on-ai-and-learning.

5
Choosing the Right Unit Model for Your Vision

Here are the foundations for the pedagogical practices discussed in this chapter:

Differentiation: It supports creating multiple pathways for learning that cater to the diverse needs, preferences, and strengths of students (Tomlinson). This aligns with the branching pathways and hybrid models, which provide flexibility and accommodate various learning styles and abilities.

Constructivism: It emphasizes learning as an active, constructive process ("Constructivism in Education"). The cycle model, where students repeatedly refine their work based on feedback, supports this theory by enabling learners to build knowledge through experience and reflection.

Zone of Proximal Development (by Vygotsky): It suggests that students learn best when new tasks are within their "zone of proximal development" and when appropriate support (scaffolding) is provided (Shabani et al.). This is evident in the hybrid and branching pathways models, which allow for tailored educational experiences that gradually extend the learner's competence.

Experiential Learning (by Kolb): It describes learning as a process where knowledge is created through the transformation of experience (Institute for Experiential Learning). This theory resonates with the cycle model's emphasis on iterative learning through doing, reflecting, and revising.

Universal Design for Learning (UDL): It advocates for designing educational environments that enable all learners to gain knowledge, skills, and enthusiasm for learning (Accessibility Resources at UNCG). The flexibility offered by the branching pathways and hybrid models supports UDL by providing multiple means of engagement, representation, and action.

Project-Based Learning: It focuses on students actively exploring real-world problems and challenges, with a process that leads to the creation of a final product or presentation (PBLWorks). The frameworks encourage students to engage deeply with content, apply what they learn, and demonstrate their knowledge through creative outputs.

Since school learning involves some kind of content, start with the linear model. How does it fit your goals? How does it fit your teaching methods? How does it fit your students' needs?

The answer might be that the linear model is all you need for a specific unit. Students may be learning something that is sequential: a step-by-step procedure. The unit may be content-heavy in vocabulary, math facts, or some other content. With this kind of learning, the linear model does the job.

But there are also use cases for branching pathway, cycle, and hybrid unit models. Student choice and flexibility? Branching pathways. Differentiation? Branching pathways. Design and testing? Cycle model. Revisiting and refining work? Cycle model. Blending individual and collaborative tasks? Hybrid model. Encouraging accountability in teamwork while maintaining individual responsibility? Hybrid model.

There are no hard and fast rules for choosing which model to use. Many times as your planning unfolds, the opportunity/need to add a branching pathway or a series of iterations or both presents itself.

The table below summarizes the four unit-structure models, highlighting their best use cases, guiding questions to help match goals to models, and practical examples from various subjects. Use this as a quick reference to determine which model—or combination of models—best fits your instructional goals, teaching methods, and students' needs.

Unit Structure	Use Cases	Questions	Examples
Linear	→ Best for content-heavy units or sequential learning. → Ideal for teaching step-by-step procedures, vocabulary acquisition, or foundational skills in any subject. → Can also work well for units where mastering each step builds toward the next.	Is the unit content-heavy or sequential, requiring mastery of specific steps? Does the material include procedures or rote learning (e.g., math facts or lab safety)?	*Language Arts*: Analyze text to produce thematic artwork and reflective essays. *Health Occupations*: Practice blood pressure measurements and write a patient education pamphlet.

(Continued)

Unit Structure	Use Cases	Questions	Examples
Branching Pathways	→ Best for units that prioritize flexibility, differentiation, or student choice. → Ideal for accommodating diverse learning styles, skill levels, or interests. → Effective for offering multiple approaches to the same goal or allowing students to evaluate different methods.	Do you want to offer flexibility in how students achieve objectives? Do students have diverse skills, preferences, or learning needs? Do you need to provide accommodations for learning disabilities? Do you want students to explore multiple methods?	*STEM*: Build an engineering prototype manually (Path 1) or with design software (Path 2). *Creative Writing*: Draft a story independently (Path 1) or use artificial intelligence (AI) to brainstorm (Path 2).
Cycle	→ Best for refining and improving work through trial, feedback, and revision. → Works in STEM or project-based learning, as well as creative disciplines like art or writing. → Ideal for skill mastery through multiple drafts, testing, or iterative practice.	Do you want students to refine skills through repeated attempts and feedback? Is the focus on improving outcomes through trial and revision? Do you want to provide structured opportunities to address mistakes and build confidence?	*Engineering*: Design and test a bridge prototype, revising after feedback. *Art*: Create a sketch, receive feedback, and refine it iteratively. *Writing*: Draft and revise essays after peer or teacher feedback.
Hybrid	→ Best for combining teamwork and individual accountability. → Ideal for big projects that benefit from both branching pathways and cycles. → Effective for gamifying learning with collaborative tasks balanced by personal responsibility. → Suitable for interdisciplinary projects.	Do students need to collaborate while also demonstrating individual skills? Does the project require both flexibility and refinement through cycles? Is the unit well-suited to combining teamwork with independent accountability?	*Language Arts*: Group analysis of *A&P* and individual work on *Through the Tunnel*. *CTE*: Teams design a recipe book + individuals prepare a dish. *Gamification*: Teams earn points for collaborative work and individual milestones in completing a larger project.

The branching pathways model allows students to choose between different methods or approaches to achieve the same learning goal. Or it lets the teacher assign different methods or approaches to achieve the same learning goal. Each pathway is designed to accommodate varying modifications, skill levels, abilities, or interests while converging at a unified output that demonstrates understanding. This model encourages flexibility, differentiation, and student agency. The key elements of the branching pathways model are:

1. **Common Start:** All students begin with shared foundational materials or activities to establish baseline knowledge (engaging input). This could include an introductory video, guided notes, or a lecture that provides the necessary context for the task.
2. **Branching Paths:** Students take different pathways based on their strengths, interests, needs, or available tools. Examples include:
   ◊ *Path 1*: A manual, hands-on approach (e.g., solving a problem step-by-step without AI tools).
   ◊ *Path 2*: A technology-supported or AI-assisted approach (e.g., using AI to analyze data or brainstorm solutions).
3. **Common Product:** Regardless of the chosen pathway, all students produce a final product that demonstrates or supports their learning. This ensures consistency in meeting learning objectives while allowing flexibility in the process.

Examples of Branching Pathways
1. **Quadratic Equations in Algebra:**
   ◊ *Path 1*: Solve equations manually using the quadratic formula.
   ◊ *Path 2*: Use AI or graphing tools to visualize and solve the equations.

◊ *Common Product*: A comparison chart highlighting the strengths and weaknesses of each method.
2. **Historical Analysis:**
    ◊ *Path 1*: Research primary sources manually, evaluating their relevance and reliability.
    ◊ *Path 2*: Use AI tools to analyze trends or patterns across multiple sources.
    ◊ *Common Product*: A multimedia presentation analyzing the historical event.
3. **Creative Writing:**
    ◊ *Path 1*: Draft a story independently from scratch.
    ◊ *Path 2*: Use AI as a brainstorming tool to generate plot ideas or character profiles.
    ◊ *Common Product*: A short story showcasing narrative techniques and creativity.

The branching pathways model offers distinct benefits to the learning process. It allows for student choice and flexibility. Students can select a pathway that aligns with their preferences or interests, increasing engagement and ownership of their learning. Teachers can differentiate to support diverse learners by offering pathways that match their skill levels or comfort zones, ensuring all students can achieve success. It affords students the opportunity to compare and evaluate multiple methods, fostering critical thinking and problem-solving skills. And it creates opportunities for collaboration and peer learning, where students can share their experiences and insights from different pathways.

When deciding whether to use branching pathways in your unit design, consider the following questions:

- ♦ Do you want to offer students flexibility in how they achieve the learning objective?
- ♦ Do your students have diverse skills or preferences that require differentiated approaches?

♦ Do you need to provide accommodations or modifications for students with learning disabilities while ensuring all students meet the same objectives?
♦ Do you want students to explore multiple methods or perspectives to achieve a deeper understanding of the content?

If the answer to any of these questions is "yes," then branching pathways is a good way to go.

The cycle model provides a powerful framework for deepening understanding and skill mastery. By focusing on repeated attempts and feedback, it encourages students to refine their work through a process of trial, error, and improvement. This iterative approach fosters a growth mindset, as students learn to view mistakes as valuable opportunities for learning and development. Teachers can scaffold the process by providing targeted feedback, enabling students to address weaknesses and build on their strengths. It also supports hands-on and experiential learning, allowing students to experiment, analyze results, and adapt their strategies. Ultimately, the cycle model empowers students to take ownership of their learning journey, promoting resilience and adaptability through repeated cycles of reflection and revision.

An example of a cycle in unit design would be a writing workshop where students draft an initial essay, receive feedback from peers or the teacher, revise their work based on that feedback, and then repeat the drafting and revision process several times until they reach a final product, continuously improving their writing with each iteration.

Other examples of using the cycle model in lesson design could include:

♦ **Science Experiment:**
Students design an experiment, conduct a trial run, analyze the results, identify potential flaws, modify their experiment based on the findings, and repeat the process to refine their methodology.

♦ **Math Problem-Solving:**
  Students attempt a challenging math problem, identify where they are stuck, receive guidance from classmates or the teacher, try again with a new strategy, and repeat until they successfully solve the problem.
♦ **Art Project:**
  Students create a preliminary sketch, receive feedback on composition and technique, make adjustments to their design, and continue iterating until they are satisfied with their final artwork.

The cycle model has benefits including deeper understanding of their work. With the iterative process, students gain a more comprehensive understanding of the subject matter. This model promotes a growth mindset by encouraging students to embrace mistakes as learning opportunities and continuously improve their skills. The cycle process allows students to actively participate in the learning process by making decisions and adjustments based on feedback.

When deciding whether to use cycle model in your unit design, consider the following questions:

♦ Do you want students to refine their understanding or skills through repeated attempts and feedback?
♦ Is the focus of the unit on improving outcomes through a process of trial, error, and revision?
♦ Do you want to provide students with structured opportunities to address mistakes and build confidence through step-by-step improvement?
♦ Are you looking for a framework that allows for flexible pacing and individualized feedback to support students with learning disabilities?

If the answer to any of these questions is "yes," then add a cycle component to your unit.

Of course, combining a branching pathways and a cycle component to a unit model gives you a hybrid model. The hybrid model works well in units where students need to collaborate while also showing what they can do on their own. It highlights teamwork and personal responsibility, making sure every student contributes to the group's success and takes ownership of their individual work. By balancing shared activities with independent tasks, the hybrid model creates a learning experience that builds collaboration, accountability, and creativity. Adding branching pathways gives students the flexibility to choose how they approach their work, which can increase engagement and make the learning feel more personal. Including the cycle model lets students refine their work through feedback and try again, helping them go deeper into the learning and improve their skills. Together, these models work even better: students get the benefits of choice and adaptability while also learning through trial and error. This combination supports different types of learners, builds confidence, and encourages critical thinking, making the hybrid model a great fit for complex, student-centered units.

The following are some examples of the hybrid model at work:

1. **English:**
   - *Collaborative Task*: Students work in groups to analyze *A&P* by John Updike, focusing on literary elements such as character development, setting, and theme. Each group creates a multimedia presentation summarizing their findings.
   - *Individual Task*: Independently, each student analyzes Doris Lessing's *Through the Tunnel* using the same literary lens as their group analysis.
2. **CTE – Culinary Arts:**
   - *Collaborative Task*: Teams research and design a recipe book section focused on regional or seasonal cuisine,

compiling recipes, cooking techniques, and cultural significance.
- ◊ *Individual Task*: Each team member selects one dish from the recipe book and prepares it independently, showcasing their skills and creativity in plating and presentation.

3. **STEM – Engineering:**
   - ◊ *Collaborative Task*: Teams design and test a bridge prototype using shared research and collaborative brainstorming sessions. Each group presents a unified plan for their prototype, including calculations and material selections.
   - ◊ *Individual Task*: Each student creates an independent report reflecting on the team's design process, discussing how their individual contributions influenced the final product and proposing improvements based on testing results.

4. **Social Studies:**
   - ◊ *Collaborative Task*: Groups create a timeline of key events leading to the Civil Rights Movement, and present their findings in a digital format.
   - ◊ *Individual Task*: Students independently research a specific individual or event from the timeline and write a detailed profile or analysis connecting it to the group's broader timeline.

5. **Art:**
   - ◊ *Collaborative Task*: Students work together to design and curate an exhibit based on a shared theme, such as "The Evolution of Perspective in Art."
   - ◊ *Individual Task*: Each student creates a personal artwork inspired by the exhibit's theme, accompanied by an artist's statement explaining how their piece connects to the collaborative exhibit.

When deciding whether to use the hybrid model in your unit design, consider the following questions:

- Do students need to collaborate while also demonstrating individual skills?
- Does the project require both flexibility and refinement through cycles?
- Is the unit well-suited to combining teamwork with independent accountability?

If the answer to any of these questions is "yes," then use the hybrid model.

Teachers can construct units in an almost unlimited number of variations. For example, unit structures can be "piggybacked" by using a creative output as a new engaging input, as shown in Figure 5.1.

The possibilities are limited only by the learning objective(s) and your imagination.

Choosing the right unit structure model is about more than just organizing content; it's about aligning your teaching goals with your students' needs and creating opportunities for meaningful learning. Whether you're using the linear model for step-by-step mastery, the branching pathways model for flexibility and differentiation, the cycle model for refining skills through iteration, or the hybrid model for blending collaboration and individual accountability, each structure offers unique strengths. By thoughtfully selecting and combining these models, you can design units that engage students, foster critical thinking, and encourage personal growth. The key is to remain flexible and responsive, adapting your approach as your planning unfolds and your students' needs evolve.

Chapter 6 is about implementing AI into the five-stage framework, offering a practical guide for teachers to decide when AI can enhance learning without undermining effort,

86 ♦ Designing Lessons in the AI-Infused Classroom

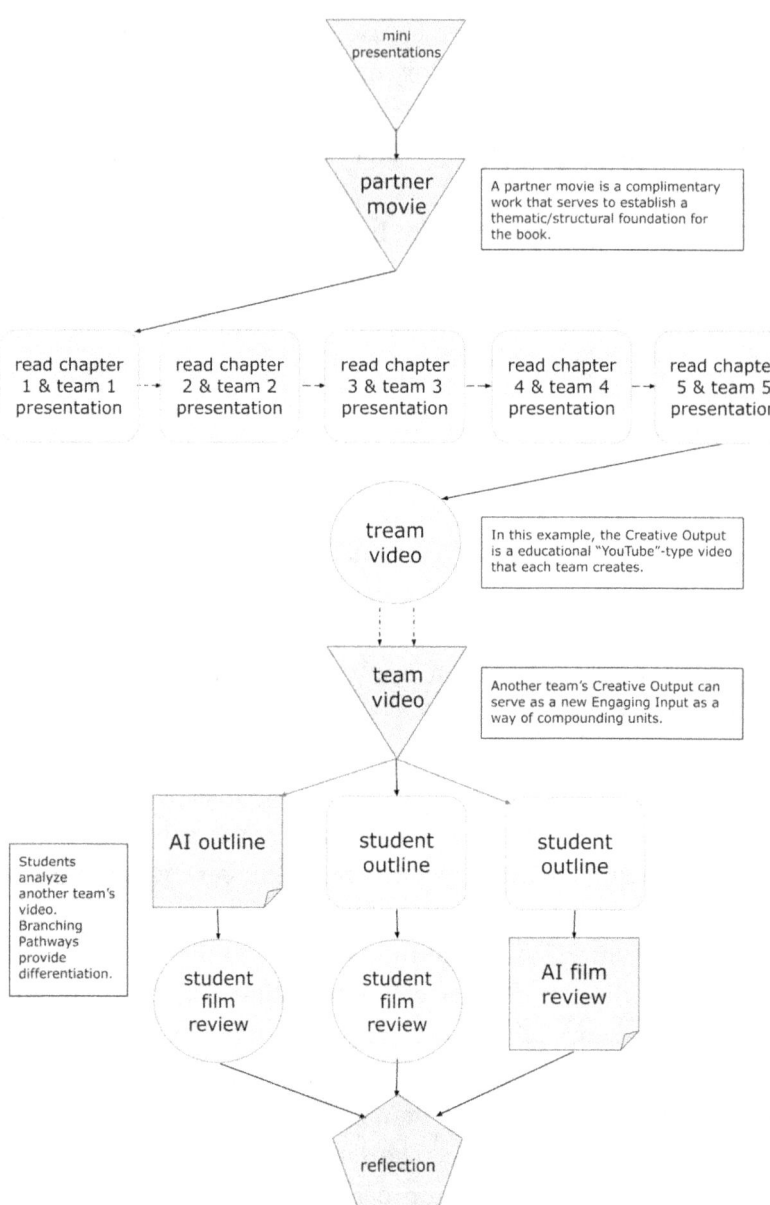

FIGURE 5.1 Literature and Video Integrated Unit Model

balance AI's strengths with student-generated work, and create AI-integrated assignments that align with the framework. This approach builds on Chapter 3's exploration of the framework by focusing on practical strategies for real-world implementation.

Chapter 5 Postscript: Ethical Considerations

Teachers need to design learning activities with these issues in mind:

- **Human Interaction:** The strategies in this chapter emphasize personalized learning experiences that AI can support but not fully replicate. It's crucial for educators to ensure that AI tools are used to enhance learning without replacing the critical elements of human interaction (such as teacher feedback and peer collaboration), which are essential for social-emotional learning (Nufer).
- **Scaffolding:** AI can help in customizing learning experiences, but AI might either oversimplify tasks or make them too challenging. Teachers should monitor and adjust AI-designed scaffolding to ensure it is effectively tailored to individual learner's needs without causing frustration or disengagement (Habib).
- **Accessibility and Inclusivity:** While AI can provide various modes of learning and assessment, there's a risk that AI applications might not be accessible to all students, particularly those with disabilities. It's important for educators to be aware that AI may not be designed with accessibility in mind. Educators may need to modify AI-produced output so that it can be used by students with a range of abilities and needs (Devon; Stravopodis).
- **Implicit Bias in AI:** Generative AI may have been trained on data that can perpetuate existing biases. These biases can

affect learning materials and methods created by AI, potentially reinforcing stereotypes. Educators need to be aware of potential biases in AI output and to use these tools critically ("Addressing Bias in AI | Center for Teaching Excellence"; "AI Biases Explained—Learn More About Them").

Works Cited

Accessibility Resources at UNCG. "Universal Design for Learning", 2025, https://accessibility.uncg.edu/for-all/udl/.

"Addressing Bias in AI | Center for Teaching Excellence." *The University of Kansas*, 2025, https://cte.ku.edu/addressing-bias-ai.

"AI Biases Explained—Learn More about Them." *Covisian*, 24 June 2024, https://covisian.com/tech-post/ai-biases-explained-learn-more-about-them/.

"Constructivism in Education." *UBC Master of Educational Technology Program*, 2015, https://constructivism512.weebly.com/meet-the-theorists.html.

Devon, Joe. "The Impact of AI in Advancing Accessibility for Learners with Disabilities." *EDUCAUSE Review*, 10 Sept. 2024, https://er.educause.edu/articles/2024/9/the-impact-of-ai-in-advancing-accessibility-for-learners-with-disabilities.

Habib, Sabrina. "AI Can Help—and Hurt—Student Creativity." *University of South Carolina*, 5 Feb. 2024, https://sc.edu/uofsc/posts/2024/02/conversation-ai-help.php.

Nufer, Sean. "Balancing Human Touch with AI in Education." *Canvas Community*, 21 Dec. 2023, https://community.canvaslms.com/t5/Artificial-Intelligence-in/Balancing-Human-Touch-with-AI-in-Education/ba-p/590952.

PBLWorks. "What Is Project Based Learning?", *Buck Institute for Education*, n.d., https://www.pblworks.org/what-is-pbl.

Shabani, Karim, et al. "Vygotsky's Zone of Proximal Development: Instructional Implications and Teachers' Professional Development." *ERIC*, 2010, https://files.eric.ed.gov/fulltext/EJ1081990.pdf.

Stravopodis, Minas. "AI and Access to Education: Bridging the Digital Divide." *IRIS Sustainable Development*, 7 Mar. 2024, https://www.irissd.org/post/ai-and-access-to-education-bridging-the-digital-divide.

Tomlinson, Carol Ann. "What Is Differentiated Instruction?" Reading Rockets, *WETA*, 2025, https://www.readingrockets.org/topics/differentiated-instruction/articles/what-differentiated-instruction.

"What Is Experiential Learning?" Institute of Experiential Learning, 2025, https://experientiallearninginstitute.org/what-is-experiential-learning/.

6
Teaching with AI. On Your Terms

Here are the foundations for the pedagogical practices discussed in this chapter:

Constructivism: It supports the idea that learners actively construct their own knowledge through experiences ("Constructivism in Education"). This chapter emphasizes AI as a tool to facilitate active learning and problem-solving, which aligns with constructivist principles.

Differentiation: It advocates for adjusting teaching strategies to meet diverse student needs (Tomlinson). This chapter discusses using AI to tailor learning experiences and provide scaffolding, supporting differentiated instruction.

Zone of Proximal Development (by Vygotsky): It focuses on providing support until learners can perform tasks independently (Shabani et al.). This chapter highlights using AI for scaffolding to assist students in reaching learning objectives they cannot achieve alone.

Cognitive Load Theory: It deals with the amount of information a learner can process at one time (Main). This chapter suggests using AI to manage and organize information, which can help reduce cognitive load and facilitate learning.

Experiential Learning: It emphasizes learning through experience ("What Is Experiential Learning?"). This chapter discusses using AI to create simulations and interactive learning experiences, aligning with experiential learning by allowing students to explore and learn through doing.

SAMR Model (by Puentedura): It considers the integration of AI at various levels, from substituting traditional methods to redefining tasks and interactions ("SAMR Model: A Practical Guide for K-12 Classroom Technology Integration"). This chapter explores how AI can enhance traditional classroom activities and bring new capabilities that were previously not possible.

TPACK Framework (Technological Pedagogical Content Knowledge): It focuses on the integration of content, pedagogy, and technology, which is crucial for effectively utilizing AI in educational settings ("The TPACK Framework Explained (with Classroom Examples)"). This chapter discusses how AI fits into the teaching context, enhancing the pedagogical strategies without overshadowing the content knowledge.

Artificial intelligence (AI) raises a lot of questions for education. Is it something that students can use as a shortcut or to cheat? Is AI another tool in the educator's toolbox? Is it the new shiny thing that we dangle in front of students to somehow get them engaged? Or is it something to be avoided, suppressed, or banned?

The premise of this book comes from the fact that AI is not going away soon. It's here to stay. And we might as well embrace it. So when it comes to using AI as part of instruction, it's best to include it for a reason. Ask yourself the following questions for the following reasons:

Reason	Question
Pedagogical Intent	♦ What is the learning objective? (pedagogy) ♦ What help do they need? (scaffolding)
Student Needs	♦ How can AI help meet the diverse needs of my students? (differentiation) ♦ Can AI reduce barriers to learning? (accessibility) ♦ Does the task need to be student-driven? (ownership)
Practical Considerations	♦ Does AI add value to the learning experience? (enhancement) ♦ Will using AI prepare students for real-world applications? (relevance) ♦ Is this task something AI does better than students? (efficiency)
Engagement	♦ Can AI enhance learning? (extension) ♦ Can I make it fun? (gamification)

Chapter 2 talked about how students can harness AI like ChatGPT as a tool to illuminate their thinking and bring their ideas to life. This chapter looks at the tool from the viewpoint of the teacher. Students will be using the tool, but you will be guiding them on where and when to use it. And as the teacher, you can have them use AI in an intentional way.

Pedagogical Intent

When we set out to plan a lesson or unit, we start with the question: What is the learning objective? When designing in the AI-infused classroom, we need to make sure that AI doesn't get in the way of that objective or water it down. Intentionally assigning the role of AI as a collaborative tool can keep the learning happening where it's supposed to be: with the student. So if the learning objective is, for example, citing evidence properly, then it makes sense to have the student be the one who cites. If students are learning to solve quadratic equations using the quadratic formula, they should perform the calculations themselves. If the learning objective is for students to analyze experimental data to draw conclusions, then students should interpret the trends and make inferences. AI can check citations for accurate formatting; AI can assist with visualizing a parabola or checking solutions; AI might help by generating a graph or organizing raw data. But when students are the learners, your job is to make sure they are the doers. Ensure that AI use aligns with the core goal of the assignment—enhancing, rather than replacing, learning.

Students will not always do something flawlessly. (If they could, then there's nothing for them to learn.) That's when you ask: What help do they need to reach the learning objective? You can use AI to provide scaffolding when students need it to address gaps in understanding or skill acquisition. For example, students can use AI to generate hints or guides for problem-solving in math or STEM assignments. Scaffolding is something we do anyway. There's nothing wrong with outsourcing scaffolding and having students learn to prompt AI for what they need:

Subject	Example
Language Arts	If the objective is citing evidence properly, students should be responsible for selecting and citing the evidence. AI can assist by organizing notes or suggesting themes.
Math	If the objective is solving quadratic equations manually, students should perform the calculations. AI can help by visualizing the parabola or verifying the solution.
Science	If the objective is analyzing experimental data, students should interpret trends and make inferences. AI can assist by organizing raw data or generating graphs.
History	If the objective is analyzing primary sources, students should interpret and synthesize the information. AI can scaffold by generating guiding questions or suggesting outlines for analysis.
CTE—Culinary Arts	If the objective is mastering knife skills, students should practice techniques directly. AI can assist by providing video demonstrations or step-by-step guides.
CTE—Carpentry	If the objective is estimating material costs, students should perform the calculations. AI can help by generating templates or organizing supply lists for reference.

If you think about it, training students to prompt AI for help is a form of self-differentiation. Students who need help from AI can seek it out, and students who don't need help don't need to ask for it.

So it's logical to ask, "Can AI reduce barriers to learning?" The obvious answer of "yes" leads to the question, "How can AI help meet the diverse needs of my students?"

Student Needs

Differentiation refers to "learning experiences in which the approach or method of learning is adjusted to meet the needs of individual students, focusing on the 'how' of personalized learning" (Culatta). Some examples of differentiation include flexible grouping, choice boards, and scaffolding.

Depending on where the learning emphasis is, AI can help differentiate how students approach learning. For example, students can be given a choice of how they want to approach a writing assignment.

Alternatively, you can directly assign different paths to your students depending on your assessment of student need.

The branching pathways structure, as shown in Figure 6.1, illustrates only one way to incorporate AI as a differentiation tool. Given that the process filter in the unit is the learning objective and therefore student driven, pathways to the creative output can be chosen to support student preference and/or need. The ways in which you can provide differentiation are perhaps limited only by your imagination and creativity.

Here are some more examples of differentiation by AI:

Content Adjustment and Accessibility

AI can help students access or modify material to fit their individual needs.

- ♦ Students use AI to create personalized prompts, simplify complex topics, or generate analogies.

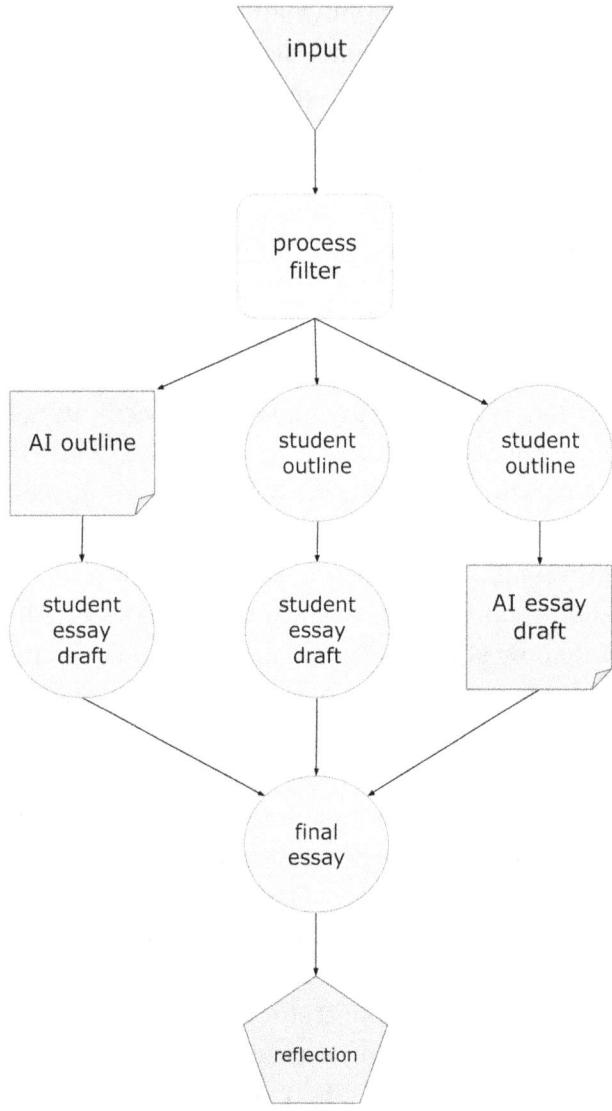

FIGURE 6.1 Essay Writing Process Options Model

- Students use text-to-speech prompts for audio versions.
- Students use AI to summarize dense material.
- AI provides multilingual translations for instructions or content, helping English language learners access the material more effectively.

Task Management and Organization

AI supports planning and organizing work.

- Students use AI to break down assignments into actionable steps, creating personalized task checklists.
- Students have AI sort or classify data for better content organization.
- Students perform a "note dump" by uploading their raw notes or brainstorming lists into AI, which organizes the information into categories, themes, or outlines to guide their next steps.
- Students use AI to create structured templates for note-taking or evidence collection to ensure all relevant details are captured systematically.

Visual and Interactive Learning

AI can engage students with visual and interactive elements.

- Students use AI to generate visual aids, such as diagrams or flowcharts, to help them better understand abstract or complex concepts.
- Students prompt AI to simulate historical figures, characters, or problem-solving scenarios to explore topics interactively.

Collaborative and Group Work

AI can foster teamwork and assign roles.

- Students prompt AI to suggest ideas for group projects, ensuring every group member has a role that matches their strengths and interests.
- Teams use AI to brainstorm, organize, or refine ideas collaboratively, ensuring that all voices are incorporated efficiently.

Practice and Feedback

AI can help students improve and self-assess their work.

- AI generates practice questions based on the content a student is studying, allowing them to test their knowledge independently.
- Students use AI to review their work and receive suggestions for improvement before submitting it to the teacher.
- Students use AI to simulate peer review by receiving suggestions on improving their work, such as clarity, organization, or depth of analysis.

AI can help meet the needs of all students by making learning more accessible, organized, engaging, and collaborative. It supports students as they take ownership of their education, helping them build on their strengths while addressing their challenges.

Practical Considerations

Students who get good at using AI technology are preparing themselves for a future in "the real world." Integrating AI into a collaborative educational experience gets them ready to be competitive and valuable in a rapidly transforming job market. So the AI-infused classroom values and teaches current and real-world technology with an eye on the future:

- Use AI to enhance student work without replacing creativity, such as generating visual aids or brainstorming ideas.
- Emphasize career-ready skills by integrating AI into collaborative tools, data analysis, or project planning.
- Use AI to suggest alternative approaches or strategies for problem-solving.
- Leverage AI for repetitive or technical tasks, like formatting citations or organizing data, freeing students to focus on higher-order thinking.

♦ Allow students to use AI for low-weighted tasks to bring their creative visions to life or produce polished products for activities not tied to core objectives.

Using AI in the classroom works best when students develop the skills to use it as a partner in their learning. Chapter 2 looked at how AI can help with tasks like organizing notes, brainstorming creative ideas, planning projects, analyzing data, and even providing feedback. The key is that students stay in control of the process, using AI as a tool to support their thinking and creativity rather than doing the work for them.

Teaching students how to write clear and thoughtful prompts is a big part of this. Good prompts help students get the most out of AI, and reviewing those prompts gives teachers a window into their thought process. It also reinforces the value of persistence and clarity in solving problems.

When students learn how to work with AI in these ways, they're building skills that will help them long after they leave the classroom. Whether they're refining an essay, organizing a project, or brainstorming ideas, they're learning how to guide AI as a collaborative partner. This approach keeps the focus on learning while preparing students for the world ahead.

Engagement

AI can push boundaries by encouraging students to explore new ideas, perspectives, or applications with AI assistance. For example, students can use AI to create interactive or game-based elements, such as quizzes, puzzles, or creative challenges, and include them as part of a student presentation. In other words, AI can help spark a student's imagination and creativity to make learning fun.

I require students to include an interactive component in their presentations. This pulls their classmates into the learning process instead of me hoping they might be passive

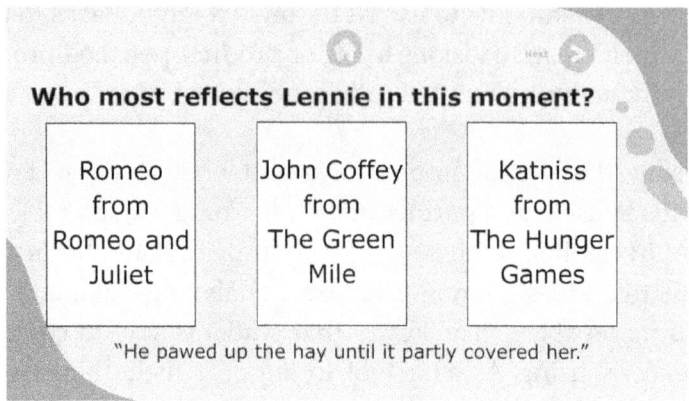

FIGURE 6.2 Character Comparison Slide

witnesses to it. And it's fun. Of course, I get Kahoots and Blookets, which are fine for what they are, but students find that ChatGPT can give ideas and suggestions for some original and quite engaging interaction. For example, a team of students was presenting on character tropes found in *Of Mice and Men*. They challenged their classmates to pick one of three characters from other stories that are similar to ones found in the book. See Figure 6.2.

It was the student's idea for the game of giving a quote from the book and asking their classmates to choose after giving a brief description of each character. ChatGPT helped pick the choices: Romeo, John Coffey, or Katniss Everdeen. The students had a vision of a game for their presentation; ChatGPT was a tool to help them achieve their vision.

Since the learning objective of the unit was to selectively collect and analyze evidence from the source (the process filter), using AI to suggest options for a learning game not only enhances that objective, but it also makes it fun. It's fun and memorable for both the presenters and the class. And as the year progresses, the idea of creative, fun, and unique presentations with games catches on—teams try to create even better experiences with their presentations.

This approach recognizes that not all tasks in the classroom carry the same instructional weight. For low-weighted assignments—like designing a board game, creating a video, or developing a fun classroom activity—AI can help students focus on their creative vision without getting bogged down in the technical details. This not only reduces the intimidation factor of large creative projects but also encourages students to explore their ideas more fully. AI becomes a tool to enhance quality and creativity, allowing students to produce polished, sophisticated outputs for tasks that increase engagement and support the learning process without replacing the effort needed to master the primary objectives. Examples of this kind of activity include:

- **Interactive Audience Engagement Tools:** Presenters use AI to help create engaging audience activities as part of their presentations.
- **Puzzle Creation:** Students prompt AI to create crossword puzzles, rebus puzzles, or word searches based on unit vocabulary or key concepts.
- **Choose-Your-Own-Adventure Activities:** Students design branching storylines or scenarios based on historical events, scientific discoveries, or literary plots.
- **Interactive Role-Playing Games:** Students use AI to script and role-play.
- **Problem-Solving Challenges:** Students can use AI to create escape room scenarios or timed challenges where students solve puzzles to "unlock" the next stage of learning.
- **AI-Enhanced Simulations:** Students can use AI to simulate real-world scenarios

That list is by no means exhaustive. Students are limited only by their imaginations, or, lacking ideas, students can prompt ChatGPT for creative suggestions. I find that if I let my students run with it, they don't let me down.

Reflection

When students use AI to help them with something, have them reflect on the process. Ask them to explain how AI supported their learning or improved their work. This gives them a context from which to evaluate the role that AI plays in their own work and learning.

Early in the school year, I introduce the AI continuum to my students. The AI continuum gives them a starting point for reflecting on their use of AI. See Figure 6.3.

There is no judgment attached to where a student places their work on the continuum other than the student's own assessment of how the tool fits into the process. It also suggests consideration of ethical use of AI in the context of schoolwork and, by extension, "real" work.

This reflection can be a quick thing, like an exit ticket. I find it easiest to just tag it on at the end of an AI-involved (or not) assignment using a Google Form. See an example in Figure 6.4.

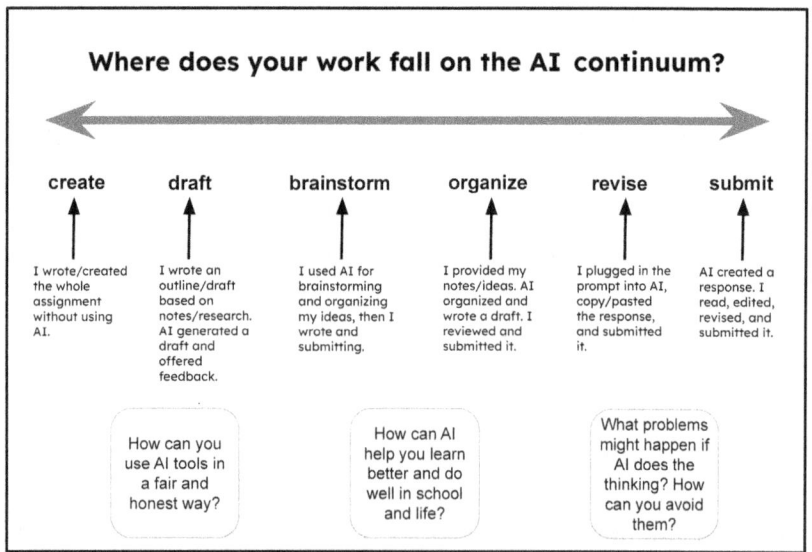

FIGURE 6.3 AI Continuum Diagram

Teaching with AI, On Your Terms ♦ 103

ChatGPT CONTINUUM REFLECTION

name *

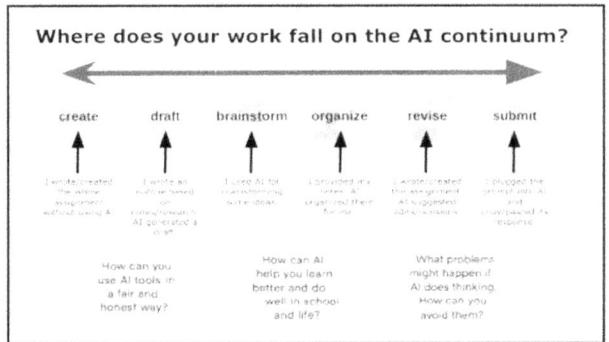

Where does your work for this assignment fall on the continuum? *

○ I wrote/created the whole assignment without using AI

○ I wrote an outline/draft based on notes/research. AI generated a draft and offered feedback.

○ I used AI for brainstorming and organizing my ideas, then I wrote and submitted.

○ I provided AI my notes/ideas. AI organized and wrote a draft. I reviewed and submitted it.

○ AI created a response. I read, edited, revised, and submitted it.

○ I plugged the prompt into AI, copy/pasted the response, and submitted it.

Explain your choice *

Your answer

Submit   Clear form

FIGURE 6.4 ChatGPT Reflection Form Screenshot

It's not a "gotcha" kind of thing. Besides the student's own learning from their reflection, it gives me valuable insight into how I'm assigning the use of AI. The following reflections are for an assignment where students gathered evidence on their own and then "dumped" their notes into ChatGPT to create an outline for an essay:

- I had AI create an outline for my essay, but I then edited a few things to make it make sense to me. I liked the way it laid the assignment out for me.
- I used AI to create the outline by pasting and tweaking my note sheet. I found it challenging to use the outline to write the essay. ChatGPT was an excellent help in figuring out how to order my sentences, though.
- I used AI for the outline and parts of the note sheet, then took those notes and used them to write the essay. I took the ideas and key points from the outline like the emotions and lyric quotes and used them to elaborate on each stage of grief. I used some outside sources for the works cited as well. I think it's really helpful using AI and helps me get my ideas out.
- I think for this particular essay AI was very useful with helping me come up with ideas for all five body paragraphs. I could've done it by myself, but it would've taken me more time to complete.

An outline is an extra step for most of my students, who do not outline as a pre-writing activity on their own. I find this kind of activity is good exposure to such a technique: They can see how it's done without the stakes being high.

AI has the potential to enhance students' learning experiences by providing scaffolding, fostering creativity, and supporting collaboration. It's a tool that can adapt to individual needs, making learning more accessible and engaging. The key is intentionality. When students use AI thoughtfully, they are active participants in their learning, leveraging technology to deepen their understanding and refine their skills.

By integrating AI in ways that align with educational goals, we prepare students not only for success in the classroom but also for a world where AI will play an ever-increasing role. Thoughtful integration keeps the focus on learning, helping students develop critical skills while embracing new possibilities.

Chapter 6 Postscript: Ethical Considerations

Teachers need to design learning activities with these issues in mind:

- **AI as a Support vs. AI as a Crutch:** There's a fine line between using AI as a support and letting it replace students' problem-solving and critical thinking skills. Teachers need to carefully manage how AI is used by students to ensure it enhances learning without undermining the development of independent learning skills. This includes setting clear guidelines for when and how AI should be used (Habib; Nufer).
- **Ensuring Equity:** Not all students may have equal access to AI technologies. Schools should strive to provide equitable access to AI for students who may be disadvantaged. This may include providing devices, ensuring accessible software, and offering training on how to use AI effectively (Devon; Stravopodis).
- **Bias in AI Algorithms:** AI systems used to generate content can perpetuate biases contained in the information trained on. Teachers need to use AI with an eye on avoiding content that can reinforce inequalities. This involves professional development (PD) so that educators can identify potential biases in AI outputs ("Addressing Bias in AI | Center for Teaching Excellence"; "AI Biases Explained—Learn More about Them")

♦ **Data Security:** The use of AI that involves the collection and analysis of student data raises concerns about privacy and data security. Educators and institutions need to ensure that student data used by AI is protected according to legal and ethical standards. This includes communicating data use policies and obtaining consent where necessary (Maddux; Soares)

Works Cited

"AI Biases Explained—Learn More about Them." *Covisian*, 24 June 2024, https://covisian.com/tech-post/ai-biases-explained-learn-more-about-them/.

"Addressing Bias in AI | Center for Teaching Excellence." *The University of Kansas*, 2025, https://cte.ku.edu/addressing-bias-ai.

"Constructivism in Education." *UBC Master of Educational Technology Program*, 2015, https://constructivism512.weebly.com/meet-the-theorists.html.

Culatta, R. "What Are You Talking about?! The Need for Common Language around Personalized Learning." *EDUCAUSE Review*, 21 Mar. 2016, https://er.educause.edu/articles/2016/3/what-are-you-talking-about-the-need-for-common-language-around-personalized-learning.

Devon, Joe. "The Impact of AI in Advancing Accessibility for Learners with Disabilities." *EDUCAUSE Review*, 10 Sept. 2024, https://er.educause.edu/articles/2024/9/the-impact-of-ai-in-advancing-accessibility-for-learners-with-disabilities.

Habib, Sabrina. "AI Can Help—and Hurt—Student Creativity." *University of South Carolina*, 5 Feb. 2024, https://sc.edu/uofsc/posts/2024/02/conversation-ai-help.php.

Maddux, Christopher. "The Importance of Student Data Privacy." *Education Technology Insights*, https://stem.educationtechnologyinsights.com/cxoinsights/the-importance-of-student-data-privacy-nid-2435.html.

Main, Paul. "Cognitive Load Theory: A Teacher's Guide." *Structural Learning*, 17 Jan. 2022, https://www.structural-learning.com/post/cognitive-load-theory-a-teachers-guide.

Nufer, Sean. "Balancing Human Touch with AI in Education." *Canvas Community*, 21 Dec. 2023, https://community.canvaslms.com/t5/Artificial-Intelligence-in/Balancing-Human-Touch-with-AI-in-Education/ba-p/590952.

"SAMR Model: A Practical Guide for K-12 Classroom Technology Integration." *PowerSchool*, 13 Apr. 2021, https://www.powerschool.com/blog/samr-model-a-practical-guide-for-k-12-classroom-technology-integration/.

Soares, Wellington. "AI Platform Use by Teachers Leads to Student Privacy Worries." *Chalkbeat*, 13 Dec. 2024, https://www.chalkbeat.org/2024/12/13/ai-tools-used-by-teachers-can-put-student-privacy-and-data-at-risk/.

Shabani, Karim, et al. "Vygotsky's Zone of Proximal Development: Instructional Implications and Teachers' Professional Development." *ERIC*, 2010, https://files.eric.ed.gov/fulltext/EJ1081990.pdf.

Stravopodis, Minas. "AI and Access to Education: Bridging the Digital Divide." *IRIS Sustainable Development*, 7 Mar. 2024, https://www.irissd.org/post/ai-and-access-to-education-bridging-the-digital-divide.

"The TPACK Framework Explained (with Classroom Examples)." *PowerSchool*, 20 Apr. 2022, https://www.powerschool.com/blog/the-tpack-framework-explained-with-classroom-examples/.

Tomlinson, Carol Ann. "What Is Differentiated Instruction?" Reading Rockets, *WETA*, 2025, https://www.readingrockets.org/topics/differentiated-instruction/articles/what-differentiated-instruction.

"What Is Experiential Learning?" Institute of Experiential Learning, 2025, https://experientiallearninginstitute.org/what-is-experiential-learning/.

7

The Architect and the Assistant
Lesson Planning with AI

Here are the foundations for the pedagogical practices discussed in this chapter:

Constructivism: It emphasizes that learners actively construct their own knowledge through experiences ("Constructivism in Education"). The chapter discusses using artificial intelligence (AI) as a collaborative tool to facilitate active learning and enhance the creation of instructional material, aligning well with constructivist principles.

Differentiation: It advocates for tailoring teaching to meet the diverse needs of students (Tomlinson). This chapter highlights using AI to create flexible learning environments and resources that can be adapted for various student needs, supporting differentiated instruction.

Zone of Proximal Development (by Vygotsky): It focuses on providing support that helps learners accomplish tasks they cannot complete independently (Shabani et al.). This chapter outlines using AI to provide scaffolding through guided prompts and structured lesson planning.

Technological Pedagogical Content Knowledge (TPACK) Framework: It emphasizes the integration of technology into teaching by intersecting technological knowledge with pedagogical and content knowledge ("The TPACK Framework Explained (with Classroom Examples)"). This chapter showcases how AI can be integrated effectively into lesson planning and material creation while maintaining educational goals.

Substitution, Augmentation, Modification, and Redefinition (SAMR) Model: It describes levels of technology integration in education ("SAMR Model: A Practical Guide for K-12 Classroom Technology Integration"). This chapter explores how AI can be used to not just substitute traditional methods but to modify and redefine the creation and delivery of educational content.

Cognitive Load Theory: It deals with managing the amount of information learners need to process simultaneously (Main). This chapter discusses using AI to streamline lesson planning and content delivery, potentially reducing cognitive load by handling complex data organization and processing.

When I'm creating lessons, I like to think of ChatGPT as a partner or an extension of myself. Somebody I can bounce ideas off of and help me turn those ideas into a plan. In Chapter 2, we talked about the student as an architect with a vision. When you're creating lessons, it's your turn to be the architect. This chapter looks at how you can use AI for planning and creating material/resources for your units.

Go into ChatGPT and prompt it with: "Write me a unit for the structure of animal cells" and it will spit out something like a

10-day unit that provides "a thorough exploration of animal cell structure, emphasizing critical thinking and real-world applications" (ChatGPT). That's great, but it's also basically something you can Google or get on one of those Teacher pay sites. Those kinds of plans may be good enough to turn in to your supervisor because lesson plans are required, but they may not be what you're looking for when you want to engage a room full of students.

This chapter takes you through the collaborative creation of a unit about using AI. Perhaps you can use the following guided unit creation as a model for your own creations.

I have an idea for a unit to explore various aspects of AI through team presentation projects. Each team researches a topic and presents its findings with an interactive presentation. Then students individually reflect on the learning experience. The learning objective is to gain knowledge and skills to successfully and ethically use AI both inside and outside of school. The skills I want students to develop are:

- writing a prompt
- using AI ethically
- using AI as an assistant
- using AI to be creative

The input is going to be a short lesson on prompt engineering and a review of Modern Language Association (MLA) basics. They need the MLA review to reinforce the notion of citing their sources. The lesson on prompt engineering will help students start thinking about moving beyond the "write the essay" kind of prompts they tend to give ChatGPT. So I want to give them some introduction to the OBJECTIVE-DETAILS-REQUEST format of the prompt.

For the process filter stage, teams research an assigned topic about using AI. The research is in preparation for making a presentation. To guide them in their work, I will provide a graphic organizer.

Their creative output will be an interactive experience (presentation) for their classmates. This ensures that students learn about all the topics, not just the one they research. Since the presentation will have an interactive component, this stage is perfect for AI integration to help students design and create some sort of activity.

Students then work on their own for the reflection. This is where they internalize what they learned in the presentations with the help of guiding questions about using AI for schoolwork and in their personal interests, and how it might benefit them in a future career.

Since student teams will be researching different topics, I will use the branching pathways model. Each team takes a different branch through the process filter stage. The unit will look something like Figure 7.1.

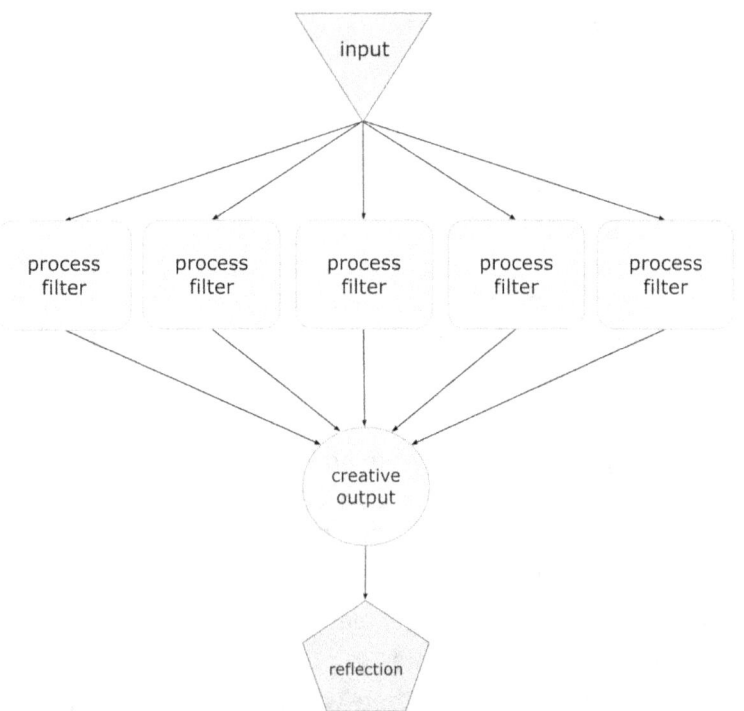

FIGURE 7.1 Multi-path Process Filter Model

I am going to use ChatGPT to help me develop this unit, so I have to think about prompting. I find with a larger task like a unit; it's virtually impossible to craft everything I need into one OBJECTIVE-DETAILS-REQUEST prompt. I do provide that information, but it comes out in the conversation with ChatGPT. I do like to start a new thread with the objective and a summary of the five-stage framework and unit structures. That gives it the context of what we're going to create:

> In this thread, you'll help me develop a unit called "AI UNIT."
>
> Below is lesson design and unit structure frameworks. We will use these frameworks.
>
> I will upload ideas and materials and text with an explanation of what it is. When I upload something, you do not need to do anything but acknowledge it; it is a resource for you. Unless/until I ask you to do or create anything, an acknowledgment is fine. Does this make sense?
>
> Universal Patterns for Lesson Design

Important note: See Appendix B for a link to the full text of lesson design and unit structure frameworks that I used in this prompt. It's a lot of text so I didn't include it here.

(You'll notice the sentence "Unless/until I ask you to do or create anything, an acknowledgment is fine." I include that in my prompts because ChatGPT likes to jump right in and spit out pages of stuff. I appreciate the enthusiasm, but I find I get lost in all of it.)

After prompting it with the thread objective and the unit/lesson context, Chat GPT will respond with something like:

> Understood! I'm ready to assist with the "AI UNIT" using the frameworks and principles you've outlined. Feel free to upload any materials or ideas whenever you're ready, and we'll proceed according to your guidance.

Now I want to tell it what my vision is:

> I have an idea for a unit to explore various aspects of AI through team presentation projects. Each team researches a topic and presents their findings with an interactive presentation. Then students individually reflect on the learning experience. The learning objective is to gain knowledge and skills to successfully and ethically use AI both inside and outside of school. The skills I want them to develop are:
>
> ♦ writing a prompt
> ♦ using AI ethically
> ♦ using AI as an assistant
> ♦ using AI to be creative

> That sounds like a comprehensive and engaging unit plan! It effectively incorporates teamwork, individual reflection, and practical applications of AI. If you have specific topics in mind for the teams to research or any particular guidelines for the interactive presentations, feel free to share those. This will help ensure the presentations align well with the learning objectives and skills you're aiming to develop.

Although it's not necessary, I like to put the brakes on the complimentary language to streamline the process. If you like it, then by all means keep it.

> Thanks for the complimentary language. Although I appreciate it, I'd prefer if you simply acknowledge any input I give you and wait for the next prompt. You don't need to offer suggestions—I will ask you for what I need when I need it.

Acknowledged. Please proceed with the next part of your unit plan whenever you're ready.

That's better. Now I'll give ChatGPT an overview of each stage of the unit. That way, when I refer to the "Process Filter" or the "Creative Output," it knows where we're heading with it.

> The input is going to be a short lesson on prompt engineering and a review of MLA basics. I want to include an interactive component.
>
> For the process filter stage, each team will research an assigned topic about using AI in preparation for making a presentation. To guide them in their work, I will provide a graphic organizer.
>
> Their creative output will be an interactive experience (presentation) for their classmates.

> In the reflection, students write about using AI for schoolwork and in their personal interests, and how it might benefit them in a future career.

> Acknowledged. If there's anything specific you need for the next steps, such as developing the graphic organizer or setting up the interactive component, just let me know!

Engaging Input

I already have the resources for the Input: Google Slide presentations of prompt engineering and the MLA review. But I want it to be a bit more engaging than straight lecture. I want to use a Google Form that they fill out while I'm presenting that gamifies the experience. Let's see what ChatGPT can do. I download the prompt engineering and MLA review presentations from Drive so they are in PDF format. Then I upload them to ChatGPT and prompt for three multiple-choice questions from each for the Google form:

> 📄 CRAFTING PROMPTS.pdf
>
> 📄 MLA RESOURCE.pdf
>
> Attached are PDFs of the lessons for the Input. I need three multiple-choice questions from each. They should be general

questions to ensure engagement with the lesson. Each question has four choices. Please provide an answer key.

Based on the content provided in the PDFs, here are three multiple-choice questions for each lesson:

For the lesson on "Crafting Prompts"

1. What is the primary objective of creating educational videos about sustainable living?
   A) To entertain viewers with fun facts
   B) To promote sustainable living practices
   C) To critique current unsustainable practices
   D) To sell sustainable products
   Answer: B

2. Which of the following is NOT listed as a topic to cover in the sustainable living videos?
   A) Composting
   B) Water conservation
   C) Solar panel installation
   D) Energy efficiency
   Answer: C

3. What should each sustainable living video include according to the assignment prompt?
   A) An interview with a celebrity
   B) Practical demonstrations and tips

C) A detailed cost analysis
D) Animation and special effects

Answer: B

For the lesson on "MLA Resource"

1. **What should the margins be set to for MLA formatting?**
   A) 0.5 inches on all sides
   B) 1 inch on all sides
   C) 1.5 inches on all sides
   D) 2 inches on all sides

   Answer: B

2. **Which of the following is necessary for an MLA-formatted Works Cited page?**
   A) Citations are arranged chronologically
   B) Citations use a hanging indent
   C) Every citation must include an abstract
   D) Citations should be single-spaced

   Answer: B

3. **How should in-text citations be formatted according to the MLA guidelines?**
   A) Author's full name and page number
   B) Author's last name or title and page number
   C) Just the page number
   D) Full website URL

   Answer: B

These questions aim to ensure engagement with the material by covering the key concepts presented in the lessons.

Okay, so the first three questions are about the example in the presentation, not about prompt engineering. Let's give ChatGPT a chance to fix it with a clarifying prompt:

> The questions from the "Crafting Prompts" PDF need to be about prompt engineering, not about the example assignment in the presentation. Can you redo those questions?

Certainly! Here are three revised multiple-choice questions focused on prompt engineering from the "Crafting Prompts" PDF:

1. **What is a key element to include when crafting a prompt for an educational assignment?**
   A) Describing the main tasks or activities involved
   B) Providing answers for potential questions
   C) Outlining penalties for incorrect answers
   D) Suggesting specific video lengths
   Answer: A

2. **Which step is crucial in the initial phase of responding to a prompt about creating a project?**
   A) Deciding the project's color scheme
   B) Stating the need for help and the context of the assignment

C) Choosing the software for presentation
D) Selecting a reward system for completion

Answer: B

3. **In crafting a prompt, what should be emphasized to ensure clarity and focus?**
A) The goal or objective of the project
B) The history of project management
C) Previous similar projects by other teams
D) The budget for the project

Answer: A

These questions aim to check the student's understanding of how to effectively create and respond to educational prompts, aligning with the goals of prompt engineering.

Now I have questions for students to answer during the lesson. To gamify it, I'll put them in a Google Form that lets students "level up" when they answer each question correctly.

Process Filter

Next I need topics, a graphic organizer, rubric, and assignment prompt for the process filter. I have five teams, so I need five topics. I have four items on my bulleted list of what I want them to learn:

- writing a prompt
- using AI ethically
- using AI as an assistant
- using AI to be creative

Let's see what ChatGPT can come up with using my list.

> I need topics for the process filter. I have five teams, so I need five topics.
>
> I have four items on my bulleted list of what I want them to learn:
>
> ♦ writing a prompt
> ♦ using AI ethically
> ♦ using AI as an assistant
> ♦ using AI to be creative
>
> Will you generate a list of five topics using my four items? Topics need to be somewhat equal in terms of researching them and presenting.

Here are five topics for the process filter stage, each designed to be equal in complexity for research and presentation by the teams:

1. **Effective Prompt Engineering: Principles and Practices**
   ◊ *Focus:* Explore the art and science of writing effective prompts for AI, including key components and techniques for clear communication.
2. **Ethical Considerations in AI Usage**
   ◊ *Focus:* Investigate the ethical implications of using AI, covering topics like bias, privacy, and accountability in various applications.

3. **Maximizing Productivity: Using AI as an Assistant**
   ◊ *Focus:* Discuss how AI can be utilized as an assistant in educational and professional settings, examining tools and strategies for enhancing productivity.
4. **Creativity and AI: Enhancing Human Creativity**
   ◊ *Focus:* Analyze how AI tools can be used to foster and enhance creativity in fields such as writing, art, and design, including examples of AI-driven creative works.
5. **Combining Skills: Writing Prompts That Leverage AI's Creative Capabilities**
   ◊ *Focus:* Develop insights on crafting prompts that specifically aim to utilize AI's creative potential effectively, including case studies and practical examples.

These topics are designed to encourage comprehensive exploration and understanding of each aspect related to AI that you've outlined, ensuring that each team has a rich subject to delve into and present.

Not bad, and the bulleted Focus sentences will work well for the assignment prompt. But I'm not sure about #5.

> The first four follow my list and are good. I need something a little more concrete than #5 for my students. Maybe something about using AI as a tutor for any subject?

Certainly! Here's a revised topic for the fifth team that focuses on a more concrete application of AI:

5. **AI as a Tutor: Personalized Learning across Subjects**
   ◊ *Focus:* Explore how AI can be utilized as a tutoring tool to provide personalized learning experiences in various academic subjects, highlighting its adaptability, responsiveness, and potential to tailor educational content to individual student needs.

This topic allows students to research and present on specific AI technologies and methodologies that support personalized education, thereby giving them a concrete and relatable use case of AI in an academic setting.

That's good. I have a graphic organizer from another unit that I want to use. I share it with ChatGPT so it knows it's part of the assignment. Figure 7.3 shows the graphic organizer filled in with example data.

ChatGPT can access a PDF and "see" the graphic organizer. That's helpful:

EXAMPLE NOTE SHEET.pdf

Students will need to cite at least one source when they research their topic. I plan to give them a blank version of the attached graphic organizer. I am showing you this document so you know it's part of the assignment.

MLA citation	Tolkien, J. R. R. The Lord of the Rings. HarperCollins, 1991.
summary	The eruption of Mount Doom, also known as Orodruin, was a cataclysmic event that occurred in the land of Mordor following the destruction of the One Ring. The Ring, a powerful and malevolent artifact created by the Dark Lord Sauron, was finally destroyed by Frodo Baggins in the fires of Mount Doom. The intense heat and pressure generated by the Ring's destruction caused Mount Doom to erupt violently, spewing forth ash, lava, and smoke. The eruption signaled the defeat of Sauron and the end of his reign of terror, as well as the conclusion of the War of the Ring.
evidence statements	"The mountain was unstable, and the heat and pressure caused by the Ring's destruction led to a violent eruption" (Gandalf 900). "The skies darkened with ash and smoke as Mount Doom spewed forth its fury, signaling the end of Sauron's reign" (Legolas 905). According to Aragorn, the eagles did not simply fly the Ring to Mount Doom due to the presence of Sauron's forces and the risk of detection (880). Samwise Gamgee noted that the eagles' involvement would have attracted too much attention and jeopardized the mission's secrecy (890). Additionally, Gandalf mentioned that the eagles were not a transportation service and had their own reasons for aiding the Free Peoples of Middle-earth (895).
media	https://www.polygon.com/23376684/lord-rings-power-lotr-mount-doom [Student inserts photo] https://www.artstation.com/artwork/OGP0ak [Student inserts photo] https://www.polygon.com/lord-of-the-rings/22432394/eagles-lotr-plot-hole-mordor [Student inserts photo]

FIGURE 7.3 Lord of the Rings Evidence Table

Acknowledged. I see the graphic organizer is part of the assignment, which will guide students in structuring their research and presentations. If there are any specific elements or instructions you need to add to the graphic organizer or any other aspect of the assignment, feel free to share those details.

I will give students a rubric for the graphic organizer. I have a rubric I used for another unit that needs tweaking. It's a little too wordy, and it's not about this topic. I can paste a screenshot of the rubric right into the prompt:

NOTE SHEET RUBRIC

Criteria	Poor (5 point)	Needs Improvement (10 points)	Good Job (15 points)
Quantity of Evidence	The note sheet has very little or incorrect information about the hero's journey parts: who the main character is, where they're going, why, the problems they face, or what they learn.	The note sheet has some information about the hero's journey, but it's missing some important parts or isn't about the main ideas.	The note sheet has a lot of good information about the hero's journey, showing that you understand what the main character goes through in the story.
Quality of Evidence	The information on the note sheet is hard to follow or doesn't really match the hero's journey parts.	The information on the note sheet is somewhat clear and mostly fits the hero's journey parts, but could be clearer or match the story better.	The information on the note sheet is clear and matches the hero's journey parts well, showing that you understand what happens in the story and its meaning.

Please rework this rubric so that it's less wordy and it's for researching an AI topic. Provide the new rubric in table format.

Here's a revised, less wordy version of the rubric adapted for researching an AI topic. The new rubric is formatted in a table:

Criteria	Poor (1 Point)	Needs Improvement (8 Points)	Good Job (15 Points)
Quantity of Information	Lacks essential details about the AI topic.	Includes basic details about the AI topic, but some key aspects are missing.	Provides comprehensive details covering all key aspects of the AI topic.
Quality of Information	Information is unclear or irrelevant to the AI topic.	Information is somewhat clear and relevant, but lacks depth or clarity in places.	Information is clear, relevant, and provides a deep understanding of the AI topic.

This revised rubric focuses on the quantity and quality of information regarding an AI topic, making it suitable for assessing student research and understanding in presentations.

> Let's make the rubric more fun. Students seem to enjoy that.

> That's good. Now change the wording to sound as if a robot is talking.

Here's the rubric revised to sound as if a robot is delivering the feedback:

Criteria	Poor (1 Point)	Needs Improvement (8 Points)	Good Job (15 Points)
Quantity of Information	Insufficient data on the AI topic is provided.	Basic data on the AI topic is present, yet it lacks comprehensive coverage.	Extensive data covering all essential aspects of the AI topic is provided.

Criteria	Poor (1 Point)	Needs Improvement (8 Points)	Good Job (15 Points)
Quality of Information	Data is unclear or not pertinent to the AI topic.	Data clarity and relevance are moderate, requiring deeper analysis and clarity.	Data is precise, pertinent, and demonstrates a thorough comprehension of the AI topic.

This version adopts a more formal, mechanical language style, fitting for a robotic voice, focusing on terms like "data" and "comprehensive coverage" to maintain a technical tone.

All I need now for the process filter is the assignment prompt. ChatGPT "remembers" everything we've done in the thread so far—including any uploaded files and images, so it can draw on all of it to write the prompt. Notice that I can just ask for the prompt knowing that it "understands" what I want to ask students to do:

> Now I need a prompt for the note sheet assignment.

Here's a prompt for the note sheet assignment crafted to sound as if a robot is instructing:

Assignment Prompt: AI Topic Research Note Sheet

Objective: Your task is to meticulously gather data on a designated AI topic, ensuring you cover all essential aspects relevant to the subject matter.

Instructions:

1. **Data Collection:** Access diverse sources to compile a comprehensive dataset on your assigned AI topic. Include books, articles, and reputable online resources.
2. **Note Sheet Completion:** Utilize the provided note sheet to record your findings. Ensure that your entries are concise, relevant, and clearly articulated.
3. **Criteria for Evaluation:**
    ◊ **Quantity of Information:** Your note sheet must exhibit a thorough collection of data, covering all necessary facets of the AI topic.
    ◊ **Quality of Information:** The data should be precise, relevant, and demonstrate your deep understanding of the topic.

Submission: Submit your completed note sheet by the specified deadline. Ensure your data is well-organized and adequately supports your understanding of the AI topic.

Assessment: Your submission will be evaluated based on the completeness and clarity of information provided, as outlined in the grading rubric.

This prompt provides clear, structured instructions in a formal tone suitable for a robotic voice, guiding the students on how to approach the assignment effectively.

Nice touch writing like a robot! I do notice that the prompt instructs students to "Access diverse sources ..." but I really only need them to consult one source for this stage of the unit. Of course, I can make revisions myself without getting ChatGPT to do it. But since ChatGPT remembers what we do as it creates more stuff in the thread, I like to get it to do the work so it remembers our revisions:

> I really only need students to consult a single online source for this stage of the unit.

Assignment Prompt: AI Topic Research Note Sheet

Objective: Your task is to extract data on a designated AI topic from one authoritative online source. Ensure the source thoroughly covers essential aspects relevant to the subject matter.

Instructions:

1. **Online Source Selection:** Identify one authoritative online resource that offers comprehensive information on your assigned AI topic. This may include digital encyclopedias, official publications, or academic databases.
2. **Note Sheet Completion:** Employ the provided note sheet to systematically record key findings from your chosen online source. Ensure that your entries are accurate, relevant, and succinctly articulated.

3. **Criteria for Evaluation:**
   ◊ **Quantity of Information:** Your note sheet must include all critical aspects of the AI topic as detailed in your source.
   ◊ **Quality of Information:** The information should be precise, pertinent, and demonstrate a clear understanding of the topic.

Submission: Submit your completed note sheet by the specified deadline. The information must be well-organized and reflect a thorough comprehension of the AI topic based on your online source.

Assessment: Your submission will be evaluated based on the relevance and clarity of information provided, as outlined in the grading rubric.

At this point, the process filter stage is ready to go. When I assign topics to teams, I'll include the topic and focus sentences in each team's assignment. I do want to add on what I call a "Quiz of Understanding" (QOU). The QOU consists of five multiple-choice questions about the assignment. I put them in a Google Form and let students take and retake until they get all five correct. Since I started doing this, students understand the expectations so much better, and I find I'm not admonishing them to read the directions. ChatGPT is really good at making QOUs:

> I need a quiz that students take to make sure they understand what to do for this assignment. Please create five multiple-choice questions with four choices for each and include an answer key. Format for a Google Form.

Here's a quiz to check for student understanding:

Quiz: Understanding the AI Topic Research Note Sheet Assignment

Instructions: Answer the following questions to confirm your understanding of the note sheet assignment requirements. Select the most appropriate answer for each question.

1. **What type of source are you required to use for the note sheet assignment?**
   A) Any source you like
   B) Multiple scholarly articles
   C) One authoritative online source
   D) Print media sources only
   Correct Answer: C

2. **What should you record on your note sheet?**
   A) Personal opinions about the AI topic
   B) Key findings from the selected online source
   C) Information from class discussions
   D) Data from various internet forums
   Correct Answer: B

3. **Which of the following best describes the quantity of information you need to include on the note sheet?**
   A) Only the most basic facts about the AI topic
   B) As much information as possible, regardless of relevance

C) Comprehensive coverage of all critical aspects detailed in the source
D) Random facts that are loosely related to the topic

Correct Answer: C

4. **How should the information on the note sheet be organized?**
   A) In a random order as found in the source
   B) Alphabetically by the source title
   C) Based on personal preference
   D) In a clear and well-organized manner reflecting the source's structure

   Correct Answer: D

5. **By when must the completed note sheet be submitted?**
   A) Anytime before the end of the semester
   B) Within a week after the assignment is given
   C) By the specified deadline in the assignment instructions
   D) After all team members have reviewed it

   Correct Answer: C

Answer Key:
1. C
2. B
3. C
4. D
5. C

These questions are designed to check the understanding of assignment instructions, focusing on critical elements such as source selection, data recording, and submission guidelines. The quiz format is suitable for a Google Form, providing clear and direct questions that ensure students grasp the requirements of the note sheet assignment.

Creative Output

The creative output is a presentation. Each team creates some kind of product (Google Slides, skit, video, etc.) based on its topic of research and showcases it to the class. The showcase needs to have an interactive component—meaning the class participates somehow. Most teams do a Google Slides presentation, but I like to let them know there are other options.

The interactive component is the same philosophy as the quiz I made for the engaging input lessons. It's something that gets the audience engaged by doing something other than being passive.

I also want teams to use AI, so I want the team to submit a link showing the thread.

> The creative output is a presentation. Each team creates some kind of product (Google Slides, skit, video, etc.) based on their topic of research and showcases it to the class. The showcase needs to have an interactive component—meaning the class participates somehow. The interactive component can be a quiz or a game—something that gets the audience engaged by doing something

> other than being passive. I also want teams to use AI, so I want the team to submit a link showing the thread.
>
> Please create a prompt for the creative output. Bullet list some suggestions for the product and another bullet list of suggestions for the interactive component.

Here is an assignment prompt for the creative output:

Assignment Prompt: Creative Output for AI Topic Research

Objective: Transform your research on AI topics into an engaging and creative presentation. This should not only inform but also actively involve your classmates in learning about the topic.

Instructions: Each team will create a product based on its AI research and include an interactive component to engage the class during the showcase. Additionally, utilize AI to assist in creating your presentation or interactive component and submit a link showing your AI thread for review.

Suggestions for the Product:
- **Google Slides Presentation:** Design a slide deck that visually presents your AI topic, enhanced by AI-generated graphics or data visualizations.
- **Skit:** Develop a scripted performance that dramatizes a concept or debate surrounding your AI topic, possibly using an AI script helper.

♦ **Video Documentary:** Produce a documentary that includes interviews, demonstrations, or narrations generated through AI tools.
♦ **Interactive Demonstration:** Create a live demo or simulation that illustrates the practical application of AI in real-world scenarios.

Suggestions for the Interactive Component:
♦ **Live Quiz:** Use an AI tool to generate quiz questions based on your presentation content, and host it using platforms like Kahoot or Quizizz.
♦ **Role-Playing Game:** Design a scenario where classmates make decisions based on AI predictions or analysis, affecting the outcome live.
♦ **Interactive Polls:** Conduct live polls using AI to analyze and present real-time data about class opinions or choices.
♦ **Q&A Session:** Implement an AI facilitator to help field and answer questions from the class in an interactive discussion.

Submission Requirements:
♦ Finalize your product and ensure the interactive component is ready for live engagement.
♦ Submit the link to your AI thread that shows how AI was used in creating your project.
♦ Be prepared to present to the class, actively involving them with your chosen interactive method.

> This prompt guides students in using AI to enhance their research presentations, ensuring they engage their peers in a dynamic and participative learning experience.

It's good, but my students need things a little simpler. So we do a tweak. Even though my students are in high school, I find that asking ChatGPT to word directions and prompts for fifth-graders helps with clarity. And gamifying it helps too.

> Please simplify the language. Make it like sending fifth-graders on a mission.

Here's the revised prompt:

Assignment Prompt: Creative Project on AI Topics

Mission: Turn your AI topic research into a super fun and interesting project! Your project should teach your classmates about your topic and include a special part where everyone gets to join in.

Instructions: Create a project that shows what you've learned about AI. Make sure there's a fun activity that gets everyone involved. Use AI to help make your project and include a link showing how you did it.

Ideas for Your Project:
- **Google Slides Presentation:** Make a colorful slideshow with cool facts and pictures about your AI topic.

- **Skit:** Put on a short play about your AI topic. You can use AI to help write your script!
- **Video Documentary:** Create a mini-movie about your AI topic using interviews and fun facts. AI can help you edit your video!
- **Interactive Demonstration:** Show something amazing about AI with a hands-on activity that everyone can try.

Ideas for Making It Fun:
- **Live Quiz:** Set up a quiz with questions about your project. You can use AI to come up with fun questions!
- **Role-Playing Game:** Make a game where classmates decide what happens next in a story about AI.
- **Interactive Polls:** Ask your classmates to vote on something during your presentation. You can use AI to analyze the results live!
- **Q&A Session:** Let everyone ask questions about your AI topic, and use AI to help answer them.

What to Turn In:
- Make sure your project and the fun activity are ready to show to the class.
- Don't forget to include the link to your AI thread that shows how you used AI to help with your project.

Your mission is to make learning about AI exciting and get everyone involved. Be creative and have fun showing your classmates how cool AI can be!

Now I need a rubric. Actually two rubrics: one for the product and one for the showcase. Students are asked to use AI to help them create the product for the creative output, so the rubric can reflect the objectives:

- using AI as an assistant
- using AI to be creative

> Please create a rubric for this activity. List criteria in the left column and have three columns for scoring, low to high. Students are asked to use AI to help them create the product for the creative output, so the rubric can reflect the objectives:
>
> - using AI as an assistant
> - using AI to be creative
>
> Please make the rubric in a table format.

Here's a rubric designed for the creative output activity, structured to assess how effectively students use AI as an assistant and to foster creativity in their project. The rubric includes criteria aligned with the objectives and provides a scoring range from low to high:

Criteria	Low (1–3 Points)	Medium (4–6 Points)	High (7–10 Points)
Use of AI as an Assistant	AI is used minimally or not effectively in the project.	AI is used adequately, assisting in some aspects of the project.	AI is used effectively throughout the project as an assistant.
Creativity in AI Application	The project shows little creativity in the application of AI.	The project shows moderate creativity in how AI is applied.	The project demonstrates high creativity in the application of AI.

Criteria	Low (1–3 Points)	Medium (4–6 Points)	High (7–10 Points)
Engagement of Audience	The interactive component fails to engage the audience.	The interactive component somewhat engages the audience.	The interactive component fully engages the audience.
Clarity and Organization of Presentation	Presentation is unclear and poorly organized.	Presentation is somewhat clear and organized.	Presentation is very clear, well-organized, and easy to follow.
Accuracy and Relevance of Content	Content has inaccuracies and is not relevant to the topic.	Content is mostly accurate and relevant to the topic.	Content is accurate, well-researched, and highly relevant to the topic.

This rubric encourages students to integrate AI effectively into their projects, not just as a tool for completing tasks but as a way to enhance creativity and engagement. The scoring criteria are designed to recognize the varying degrees of success in using AI, engaging the audience, and presenting information clearly and relevantly.

That's pretty good. I don't think I want to include the "Creativity in AI Application" criteria. Students are beginning to learn how to use AI, and "high creativity" may be hard to define. I think the creativity I'm looking for with this project will reveal itself in the other criteria.

Please remove the "Creativity in AI Application" row.

Here's the revised rubric with the "Creativity in AI Application" row removed, focusing on the use of AI as an assistant, audience engagement, clarity and organization of the presentation, and the accuracy and relevance of the content:

Criteria	Low (1–3 Points)	Medium (4–6 Points)	High (7–10 Points)
Use of AI as an Assistant	AI is used minimally or not effectively in the project.	AI is used adequately, assisting in some aspects of the project.	AI is used effectively throughout the project as an assistant.
Engagement of Audience	The interactive component fails to engage the audience.	The interactive component somewhat engages the audience.	The interactive component fully engages the audience.
Clarity and Organization of Presentation	Presentation is unclear and poorly organized.	Presentation is somewhat clear and organized.	Presentation is very clear, well-organized, and easy to follow.
Accuracy and Relevance of Content	Content has inaccuracies and is not relevant to the topic.	Content is mostly accurate and relevant to the topic.	Content is accurate, well-researched, and highly relevant to the topic.

This version of the rubric streamlines the assessment criteria to focus more specifically on the practical use of AI and the effectiveness of the presentation itself.

Now all I need is a rubric for the showcase portion of the creative output. I like to keep that pretty simple with criteria of speaking skills and organization. Do the presenters speak clearly and look at the audience? Is the presentation structured with a clear beginning, middle, and end?

> I need a rubric for the showcase portion of the Creative Output. Let's do two criteria of speaking skills and organization. Do the presenters speak clearly and look at the audience? Is the presentation structured with a clear beginning, middle, and end? Use the same column format as the previous rubric.

Here's a rubric specifically designed for assessing the showcase portion of the creative output, focusing on speaking skills and organization of the presentation:

Criteria	Low (1–3 Points)	Medium (4–6 Points)	High (7–10 Points)
Speaking Skills	Presenters mumble, speak too quietly, or fail to make eye contact with the audience.	Presenters speak clearly but occasionally fail to make eye contact or engage the audience.	Presenters speak clearly and consistently make eye contact, effectively engaging the audience.
Organization	Presentation lacks a clear structure; beginning, middle, and end are not discernible.	Presentation has a recognizable beginning, middle, and end but transitions may be rough.	Presentation is well-structured with a clear beginning, middle, and end, and smooth transitions.

This rubric provides a framework for evaluating how well students deliver their presentations and how effectively they organize their content. It emphasizes clear communication and structured presentation, which are critical for engaging and informing an audience effectively

Since the students include an interactive component to their presentations, I don't need to provide one myself (like the "quiz" I made for the engaging input stage).

Reflection

This final stage of the framework allows students to internalize the material that the teams uncovered. I'm thinking about a short paper (two pages max + Works Cited) to talk about how the skills and knowledge students gained in this unit apply to them both inside and outside of school. Since we've been using and citing evidence all year, I want them to continue the practice using evidence statements from at least two supplied articles about teens and AI. Or they can use sources they find themselves. I want to include guiding questions, a rubric, and a QOU.

Just to double check to make sure I'm seeing the big picture, I'll run it by ChatGPT before we create the materials:

> For the reflection, I want to assign a short paper (two pages max + Works Cited) to talk about how the skills and knowledge students gained in this unit apply to them both inside and outside of school.
>
> Since we've been using and citing evidence all year, I want them to continue the practice using evidence statements from at least two supplied articles about teens and AI. Or they can use sources they find themselves. To guide their reflection, I want to give them questions about:
>
> - How the information they learned changed the way they approach schoolwork.
> - How the AI skills and knowledge they learned can be useful in managing your personal tasks or hobbies?
> - How the understanding and experience with AI you gained in this unit might benefit their future career?
> - How this unit has changed your perspective on AI and its role in society?
>
> I will supply a rubric and a QOU.
>
> Is there anything you think I need to add or remove? Keep in mind the learning objectives for this unit.

Your reflection assignment structure and guiding questions are well-aligned with the learning objectives of understanding and applying AI skills both academically and personally. Here are a few considerations to ensure the assignment is comprehensive and effective:

1. **Clarify Evidence Requirements:** You've mentioned that students should use evidence statements from at least two supplied articles or find their own sources. It might be helpful to explicitly state how many pieces of evidence you expect them to incorporate per question or in total to ensure they engage deeply with the sources.
2. **Guidance on Citing Sources:** Since the paper requires a Works Cited page, providing a brief reminder or resources on proper citation formats (especially if they use AI-generated content) would reinforce good academic practices.
3. **Integration of Personal Reflection:** Ensure that the questions explicitly prompt students to reflect personally. This could be emphasized by rephrasing questions slightly, for example:
    ◊ "How has the information you learned changed your approach to schoolwork and personal tasks?"
    ◊ "In what ways can the AI skills and knowledge you've acquired assist you in your hobbies or daily tasks?"

4. **Examples of AI Application:** It might be beneficial to provide or suggest specific scenarios or examples of how AI can be used in various fields or hobbies. This would help students think more concretely about how to apply their knowledge.
5. **Discussion on Ethical Considerations:** Considering the unit's focus on AI, adding a question or a section about the ethical implications of AI use could deepen students' understanding of AI's societal impacts.
6. **Feedback Mechanism:** Since this is a reflective assignment, consider how you will provide feedback. Will there be a peer review component, or will you give individual feedback? Clarifying this can help students understand the value of reflection and feedback in learning.

If the reflection paper and its components align well with these considerations, it should effectively meet your unit's learning objectives. If you plan to add a peer review or discussion component, it might also enhance the learning experience by allowing students to engage with and reflect on their peers' perspectives on AI.

These are helpful suggestions. I'm going to pass on #1 and #2 since using evidence is and will be an ongoing skill that they are developing. I prefer to give feedback rather than make it a requirement (but that's just me). I will have ChatGPT rephrase guiding questions when it does the assignment prompt. The fourth comment doesn't fit well with what they were asked to research. I will have ChatGPT include #5 since that's one of the objectives as well as one of the topics. Finally, students are already familiar with my feedback methodology of increasingly specific comments and multiple opportunities for revision (again, that's me).

> Please revise. Change the 4 "content requirements" to guiding questions. Remove the third bullet from #3. Move #2 and #3 into the objective section as regular text. Delete #4.

Assignment Prompt: Reflective Paper on AI Learning Experience

Objective: Write a two-page reflection paper to explore your personal experience with AI during this unit. In your paper, address the following guiding questions:

- How has the information you learned changed your approach to schoolwork and personal tasks?
- In what ways could the AI skills and knowledge you've acquired assist you in managing your personal tasks or hobbies?
- How might the understanding and experience with AI gained in this unit benefit your future career?
- How has your perspective on AI and its role in society evolved, especially considering ethical considerations?

Support your reflections with evidence from at least two articles provided about teens and AI, or from credible sources you find yourself. Incorporate at least one piece of evidence per question to substantiate your reflections. Use MLA format for your paper and citations.

Submission: Submit your paper through the designated digital platform by the due date provided.

This assignment encourages you to critically reflect on how AI influences various aspects of life, connecting classroom learning with real-world applications and ethical considerations.

Of course, if you want peer review or guidance on citing sources, that's your vision. You know your students, and you know where you're taking them.

Let's finish this unit. Rubric, then QOU.

Please create a rubric for this assignment. Use the same rubric table setup. Use these four criteria:
- Analysis
- Content
- MLA
- Mechanics

Here's a rubric designed to evaluate the reflective paper on AI learning experiences, focusing on the criteria of Analysis, Content, MLA format, and Mechanics:

Criteria	Low (1–3 Points)	Medium (4–6 Points)	High (7–10 Points)
Analysis	Provides minimal analysis, with superficial reflections.	Offers moderate analysis with some depth in reflections.	Demonstrates thorough and insightful analysis with deep reflections.
Content	Content lacks relevance, detail, or is minimally developed.	Content is generally relevant and adequately developed.	Content is highly relevant, well-developed, and thoroughly supported by evidence.
MLA Formatting	Numerous errors in MLA formatting and citation style.	Some inconsistencies with MLA formatting and citation style.	Adheres strictly to MLA formatting and citation guidelines with no errors.
Mechanics	Frequent grammatical, spelling, or punctuation errors.	Occasional grammatical, spelling, or punctuation errors.	Virtually no grammatical, spelling, or punctuation errors.

This rubric ensures that each aspect of the assignment—from the depth of analysis to the precision of writing and adherence to formatting rules—is carefully assessed, providing clear criteria for achieving high marks.

You forgot to include some of the things from the assignment prompt: citations, works cited, maximum number of pages, all four guiding questions discussed, at least two sources, at least one piece of evidence per question. Fit everything in the four criteria I provided.

Here's a revised rubric that integrates the specific requirements from the assignment prompt, ensuring each aspect is addressed within the four established criteria of Analysis, Content, MLA, and Mechanics:

Criteria	Low (1–3 Points)	Medium (4–6 Points)	High (7–10 Points)
Analysis	Minimal reflection on the guiding questions; lacks depth. Uses no or only one source.	Moderate reflection on most guiding questions; some depth. Uses at least two sources but may lack evidence for some questions.	Comprehensive and insightful analysis on all guiding questions. Uses at least two sources with evidence for each question.
Content	Content lacks relevance, detail, or is minimally developed. Fewer than four guiding questions discussed.	Content is generally relevant and adequately developed. At least three guiding questions discussed.	Content is highly relevant, well-developed, and thoroughly addresses all four guiding questions.
MLA Formatting	Numerous errors in MLA formatting and citation style. Incomplete or incorrect Works Cited page.	Some inconsistencies with MLA formatting and citation style. Works Cited page mostly complete.	Adheres strictly to MLA formatting and citation guidelines with no errors. Correct and complete Works Cited page.
Mechanics	Frequent grammatical, spelling, or punctuation errors. Paper exceeds two pages.	Occasional grammatical, spelling, or punctuation errors. Paper is exactly two pages.	Virtually no grammatical, spelling, or punctuation errors. Paper is within the maximum two-page limit.

This rubric ensures comprehensive coverage of the assignment's requirements, including the discussion of all guiding questions, proper use of sources and evidence, adherence to MLA standards, and the maintenance of mechanical accuracy within the specified page limit. It provides clear benchmarks for assessing the quality and completeness of the reflective paper.

Finally, I need a QOU. Before you create it, let me know if you remember what it is and what the specifications are.

Yes, I remember the Quiz of Understanding (QOU). It's designed to ensure students have comprehended key aspects of an assignment or unit. The quiz usually consists of multiple-choice questions, each with several answer choices. The specifics for creating this quiz typically include:

♦ Limiting the number of questions to about five.
♦ Covering the main points or instructions of the assignment to verify that students understand what is expected of them.

If you need a QOU created for this reflective paper assignment, I can draft questions that focus on verifying students' understanding of the assignment requirements and key elements you've outlined. Would you like to proceed with this, and do you have any specific points you want the QOU to cover?

Yes. Proceed.

Here's a QOU designed to ensure students have grasped the key requirements and elements of the reflective paper assignment on AI learning experiences:

Quiz: Understanding the Reflective Paper Assignment on AI Learning Experiences

Instructions: Select the correct answer for each question to demonstrate your understanding of the reflective paper assignment.

1. How many pages should your reflective paper be, excluding the Works Cited page?
   A) One page
   B) Two pages
   C) Three pages
   D) No page limit

   Correct Answer: B

2. How many sources must you use at a minimum for your reflective paper?
   A) One source
   B) Two sources
   C) Three sources
   D) Four sources

   Correct Answer: B

3. What must be included in your paper according to MLA guidelines?
   A) A title page
   B) In-text citations and a Works Cited page
   C) An abstract
   D) A cover letter

   Correct Answer: B

4. How many guiding questions should your reflective paper address?
   A) Two
   B) Three
   C) Four
   D) Five

   Correct Answer: C

5. What is the maximum number of grammatical, spelling, or punctuation errors acceptable for the highest score in mechanics?
   A) Zero errors
   B) One to two errors
   C) Three to four errors
   D) Five or more errors

   Correct Answer: A

This QOU covers the basic structural requirements, source usage, formatting guidelines, content expectations, and mechanics of the assignment. It's designed to ensure students understand the assignment details before they begin working on their papers.

Hopefully, you're getting a sense of how using ChatGPT to create materials for a unit lets you take on the "architect" role by freeing you from the minutiae of doing tedious taskwork. In this example unit, ChatGPT is using my ideas, thinking, materials, and input to provide an informed first draft of materials that I can evaluate and then accept, modify, and/or reject. When I'm not invested in forming every word and sentence, changing or rejecting those things is so much easier. Creation and revision follows my vision and train of thought, providing almost instantaneous gratification while requiring little grunt work on my part.

Chapter 7 Postscript: Ethical Considerations

Teachers need to design learning activities with these issues in mind:

- **Content Accuracy and Appropriateness:** When AI is used to generate content, there's a risk of inaccurate or inappropriate content slipping through. Teachers should verify the accuracy and appropriateness of AI-generated content before using it in the classroom ("AI Biases Explained—Learn More about Them").
- **Overdependence on Technology:** Relying heavily on AI for lesson planning and material creation can potentially lead to a reduction in the skills educators develop, such as adapting lessons "on the fly." While AI can significantly enhance efficiency and creativity in lesson planning, teachers need to maintain a balance between AI tools and their own pedagogical skills so as not to lose the human elements of teaching (Habib; Nufer).
- **Accessibility:** Schools and educators must ensure that AI tools used in education are accessible to all students. This might involve providing necessary hardware and offering alternative ways to participate for those who cannot access AI tools (Devon; Stravopodis).

Works Cited

"AI Biases Explained—Learn More about Them." *Covisian*, 24 June 2024, https://covisian.com/tech-post/ai-biases-explained-learn-more-about-them/.

ChatGPT. "Unit Title: Exploring the Microcosm: The Structure of Animal Cells." *ChatGPT*, OpenAI, 15 Jan. 2025, https://chatgpt.com/share/6787f4d5-f8f4-8001-bbd9-8857dc47652e.

"Constructivism in Education." *UBC Master of Educational Technology Program*, 2015, https://constructivism512.weebly.com/meet-the-theorists.html.

Devon, Joe. "The Impact of AI in Advancing Accessibility for Learners with Disabilities." *EDUCAUSE Review*, 10 Sept. 2024, https://er.educause.edu/articles/2024/9/the-impact-of-ai-in-advancing-accessibility-for-learners-with-disabilities.

Habib, Sabrina. "AI Can Help—and Hurt—Student Creativity—USC News & Events." *University of South Carolina*, 5 Feb. 2024, https://sc.edu/uofsc/posts/2024/02/conversation-ai-help.php.

Main, Paul. "Cognitive Load Theory: A teacher's guide." *Structural Learning*, 17 Jan. 2022, https://www.structural-learning.com/post/cognitive-load-theory-a-teachers-guide.

Nufer, Sean. "Balancing Human Touch with AI in Education." *Canvas Community*, 21 Dec. 2023, https://community.canvaslms.com/t5/Artificial-Intelligence-in/Balancing-Human-Touch-with-AI-in-Education/ba-p/590952.

"SAMR Model: A Practical Guide for K-12 Classroom Technology Integration." *PowerSchool*, 13 Apr. 2021, https://www.powerschool.com/blog/samr-model-a-practical-guide-for-k-12-classroom-technology-integration/.

Shabani, Karim, et al. "Vygotsky's Zone of Proximal Development: Instructional Implications and Teachers' Professional Development." *ERIC*, 2010, https://files.eric.ed.gov/fulltext/EJ1081990.pdf.

Stravopodis, Minas. "AI and Access to Education: Bridging the Digital Divide." *IRIS Sustainable Development*, 7 Mar. 2024, https://www.irissd.org/post/ai-and-access-to-education-bridging-the-digital-divide.

"The TPACK Framework Explained (with Classroom Examples)." *PowerSchool*, 20 Apr. 2022, https://www.powerschool.com/blog/the-tpack-framework-explained-with-classroom-examples/.

Tomlinson, Carol Ann. "What Is Differentiated Instruction?" *Reading Rockets*, WETA, 2025, https://www.readingrockets.org/topics/differentiated-instruction/articles/what-differentiated-instruction.

8
Creating without Limits
AI in the Hands of Teachers

Here are the foundations for the pedagogical practices discussed in this chapter:

Constructivism: It supports the concept of learners actively constructing their own knowledge through interaction and creation ("Constructivism in Education"). This chapter discusses using artificial intelligence (AI) to create engaging, student-centered learning experiences, which is a core principle of constructivism.

Differentiation: It advocates for tailoring instruction to meet the diverse needs of students (Tomlinson). This chapter highlights using AI to customize learning materials and activities, thereby supporting the varied learning styles and abilities of students.

Experiential Learning: It emphasizes learning through direct experience ("What Is Experiential Learning?"). This chapter describes how AI can be used to simulate real-world scenarios or create interactive tasks that provide experiential learning opportunities.

Technological Pedagogical Content Knowledge (TPACK): It focuses on the integration of technology into teaching and learning processes ("The TPACK Framework Explained (With Classroom Examples)"). This chapter illustrates how AI can be effectively combined with pedagogical strategies and content knowledge to enhance educational outcomes.

Substitution, Augmentation, Modification, and Redefinition (SAMR) Model: It details different levels of technology integration ("SAMR Model: A Practical Guide for K-12 Classroom Technology Integration"). This chapter explores how AI can be used not just to substitute traditional methods but to augment, modify, and potentially redefine educational activities.

Universal Design for Learning: It advocates designing educational environments that enable all learners to gain knowledge, skills, and enthusiasm for learning ("Universal Design for Learning | Accessibility Resources at UNCG"). This chapter's emphasis on using AI to create flexible and accessible learning tools aligns with the UDL principles.

Cognitive Load Theory: It deals with how learners process new information and manage cognitive resources (Main). This chapter discusses using AI to design learning activities that manage cognitive load effectively, making learning more efficient and enjoyable.

The previous chapter had some examples of AI-created materials that enhance the unit. AI can partner with you to help you achieve your vision for your classroom assignments by creating materials, planning activities, and supporting collaborative projects. Many of the limits on available resources have been made obsolete by AI such as ChatGPT. In fact, you are limited only by your imagination. With a basic knowledge of how to prompt, you can use ChatGPT to help you:

- create structured prompts to guide students in using ChatGPT for tasks like narrowing topics, generating themes, or connecting evidence to key ideas.
- develop graphic organizers and note-taking templates to help students organize evidence systematically while engaging with texts or films.
- brainstorm ideas for menu choice boards, like dioramas, thematic collages, or multimedia projects.
- draft and refine rubrics for grading assignments like reflections, presentations, and creative products.
- design interactive and gamified activities, such as quizzes, role-playing scenarios, or team-based challenges.
- create frameworks for group projects where students could use ChatGPT collaboratively, such as brainstorming shared ideas or organizing research contributions.
- generate comments for feedback on assignments and projects.
- create personalized resources tailored to individual student needs, such as simplifying complex texts, generating analogies, or adjusting reading levels.
- generate multiple-choice quizzes or short-answer questions to enhance engagement and to ensure students understood learning objectives and task requirements.
- revise and polish instructional materials, such as step-by-step guides or assignment instructions, to make them more student-friendly.
- craft reflection prompts and frameworks with ChatGPT to encourage students to evaluate their own learning process, including how AI supported their work.
- have students create their own engaging input material.

This list can go on and on, and a chapter of examples might be endless. I do have, however, some real-world examples to share from my English classroom that will hopefully spark your thinking about your own lessons with your own students.

Mini-presentations

For some units we do what I call mini-presentations. That's where we do an overview of background material to create a context for a book or a play. For example, before diving into Shakespeare's Romeo and Juliet, students benefit from learning about Shakespeare, plot, characters, etc. I assign a topic and one slide of a Google Slides presentation for the "mini-presentation." I worked with ChatGPT to come up with a list of topics:

Mini-presentation Topics

1. **Shakespeare's Life:** A brief overview of who Shakespeare was, when he lived, and why he's important.
2. **The Globe Theatre:** What it was like TO watch a play in Shakespeare's time and how it influenced his works.
3. **Elizabethan England:** Key aspects of the time period that shaped Shakespeare's plays.
4. **The Language of Shakespeare:** An introduction to Shakespearean language, including iambic pentameter and unusual word order.
5. **The Plot of Romeo and Juliet:** A summary of the play's main events and conflicts.
6. **Themes in Romeo and Juliet:** Love, family conflict, fate, and other key themes in the play.
7. **The Characters in Romeo and Juliet:** Who's who in the story and their roles in the plot.

8. **Shakespeare's Influence on Literature:** How his works have shaped storytelling over the centuries.
9. **Shakespeare in Modern Times:** Why we still read and watch Shakespeare today.
10. **Adapting Shakespeare to Film:** Challenges and creative decisions directors face when adapting a play to the screen.
11. **Changing the Setting:** How setting (time and place) can change the meaning or impact of a Shakespeare story.
12. **Changing the Time Period:** Why directors might update the time period and what it adds to the story.
13. **Modernizing Language:** The pros and cons of keeping Shakespearean language versus modernizing it.
14. **Casting Choices:** How different actors' portrayals can change how characters are understood.
15. **Music in Adaptations:** How music can set the tone or highlight themes in a Shakespeare adaptation.
16. **Famous Adaptations of Romeo and Juliet:** Examples like the 1968 Zeffirelli version or the 1996 Baz Luhrmann version.
17. **Cultural Retellings:** How stories like *West Side Story* have reimagined *Romeo and Juliet* for different audiences.

I assign the topic and slide number with scratch-off tickets. I make them myself using scratch-off stickers. Gamifying it this way engages them by making them feel like they "won" something. See Figure 8.1.

Then I give them the assignment prompt:

> Let's practice our awesome presentation skills! (Not reading the slides, not a lot of text, etc.) In preparation for Romeo and Juliet, by William Shakespeare, we're going to do a bunch of mini-presentations with background information.

ROMEO & JULIET LOTTERY

Ancient Grudges

Scratch off to get your Slide number and topic.

FIGURE 8.1 Romeo & Juliet Lottery Slide

These are individual presentations. You'll get a number at random. The attached file has topics on numbered slides. The slide with your number on it is your slide. Find your topic, research it, and create about a one-minute presentation on your slide. Make sure your presentation:

- is about your assigned topic
- is like one minute long
- is well done
- credits your source(s)

After students make their slides but before they present, I have ChatGPT make a quiz (just like in the last chapter) with one multiple-choice question per slide. Students then explain their slides when they come up on the screen (they can even stay in their seats!), and the class answers the question on their Chromebooks.

Content in Different Forms

Something ChatGPT is really good at is generating content in different forms. For example, take the meme shown in Figure 8.2.

Let's use this meme as engaging input for a unit on cell biology. ChatGPT can explain what the meme is talking about and why it's funny:

> This meme uses the "car swerving onto the exit ramp" format to make a joke about mitochondria. The car, labeled "Mitochondria," should stay on the highway toward "Adenosine Triphosphate Synthesis," which is the actual process mitochondria perform to make cellular energy. Instead, the car swerves off toward the shortcut label "Powerhouse of the cell," which is the simple phrase most people remember. The humor comes from showing how we often choose the easy nickname instead of the more accurate scientific explanation.

FIGURE 8.2 Biology Meme with Mitochondria

It can explain it to a fifth-grader:

This picture is like a silly road sign. The car is called "Mitochondria," which is a tiny part of a cell that makes energy. The car is supposed to go straight toward "Adenosine Triphosphate Synthesis," which is the real science way of saying how energy is made. But instead, the car quickly turns off toward the easier nickname: "Powerhouse of the cell." It's funny because it shows how we like to use the short, simple name instead of the harder science words.

It can make it a conversation:

Alex: Have you seen that meme with the car swerving onto the exit ramp?
Jamie: Yeah, the one where the car suddenly turns instead of staying on the highway?
Alex: Exactly! In this one, the car is "Mitochondria."
Jamie: Oh, like from science class—the part of the cell that makes energy?
Alex: Yep. The highway is labeled "Adenosine Triphosphate Synthesis," which is the real process mitochondria do.
Jamie: And the exit?
Alex: "Powerhouse of the cell"—the easy name everyone remembers.
Jamie: Haha, so it's like mitochondria ditch the science words and just go for the nickname.

It can make it a rap:

(Verse)
Mitochondria drivin', straight down the lane,
ATP Synthesis, that's the real game.

But hold up—swerve, take the quick sell,
Exit ramp screamin': "Powerhouse of the cell!"

(Hook)
It's the nickname we know, the shortcut we tell,
But the science runs deeper, inside every cell.
From ATP makin' to energy flow,
Mitochondria's the engine—we all gotta know.

It can write it as a scene from a Shakespeare play:

Scene: A roadway within the kingdom of the Cell. A carriage, marked Mitochondria, veers suddenly toward the exit.

Mitochondria:
Straight on lies noble Adenosine Triphosphate Synthesis,
The labor true, whereby life's power is wrought.
Yet lo! Yon sign proclaimeth "Powerhouse of the cell,"
A simpler name, though lacking depth of thought.

Chorus:
Thus swerves the carriage, drawn by mortal tongue,
From learned truth to nickname oft-times sung.

(Exunt)

How about a sonnet?

Upon the road where mitochondria steer,
ATP Synthesis shines bright and clear.
Yet sudden swerving, quick the exit calls,
"Powerhouse of the cell" adorns the walls.
The truth lies deeper, science well-defined,

But catchy words so quickly flood the mind.
Though processes complex sustain the whole,
We cling to nicknames easier to extol.

Or a sales pitch:

Step right up! Why bother with long science words when you can have the shortcut? Forget "Adenosine Triphosphate Synthesis"—try "Powerhouse of the cell!" Easy to say, easy to remember. Sure, mitochondria do the complicated work behind the scenes, but why not take the quick exit? It's energy made simple! It's a no-brainer, trust me!

Or a movie poster.

UNLEASH THE POWER WITHIN

MITOCHONDRIA: THE POWERHOUSE EXIT
In a world where energy must be made, one cell part takes the fast lane. Will it follow the science toward Adenosine Triphosphate Synthesis, or take the quick exit to the nickname everyone knows?
A high-speed chase through the biology of life!

COMING SOON TO A MICROSCOPE NEAR YOU!

A process filter can extract the same information from different sources when the sources are generated in a deliberate and intentional manner. Regardless of the subject or the content, using multiple forms is an engaging way to introduce content to students.

YouTube Quiz

Yet another way to use AI to produce material is a YouTube quiz. Similar to the mini-presentation quiz and the Quiz of Understanding, the YouTube quiz ends up on a Google Form. Google Forms let you embed a YouTube video right in the form, as shown in Figure 8.3.

Then you get the transcript from the YouTube page, and copy/paste it into ChatGPT, as shown in Figure 8.4.

Prompt it for the quiz you want, and it will create questions based on the video transcript.

Figure 8.5 shows the questions in the Google Form.

Many plays and sonnets.
2:03
Shakespeare died in 1616 at the age of 52.
2:08
To this day, audiences enjoy attending his plays, and today
2:13
Shakespeare's stories are being remade into movies,
2:17

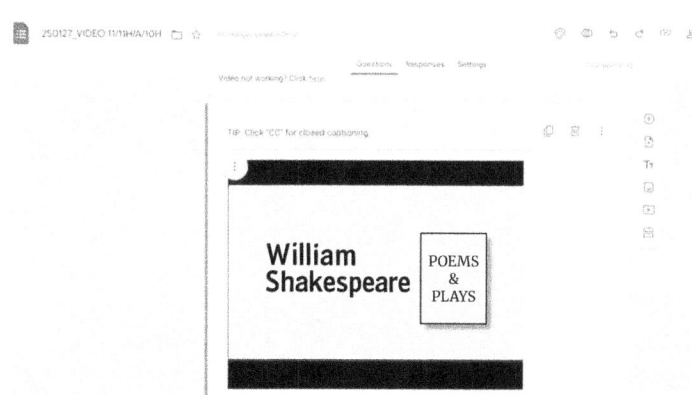

FIGURE 8.3 Shakespeare Video Quiz Editor Screenshot

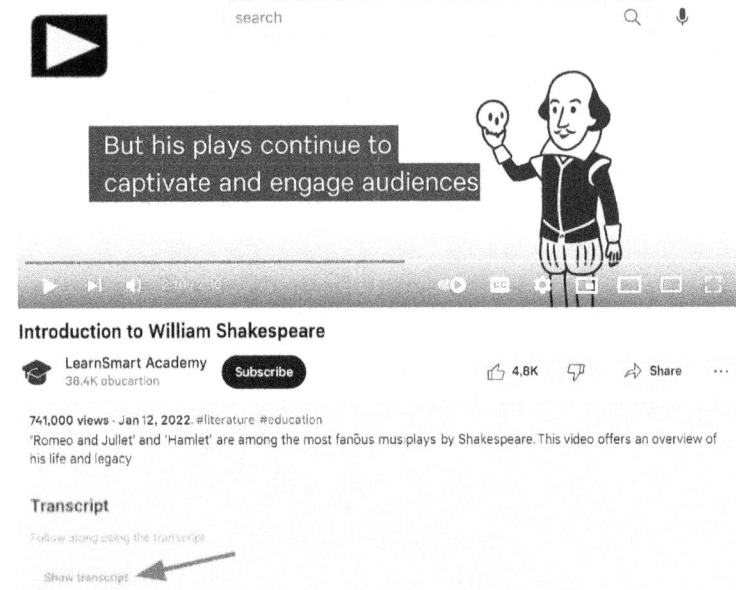

FIGURE 8.4 Shakespeare YouTube Video Screenshot

books and even music.
2:20
You don't have to be an academic type to enjoy Shakespeare.

Google Form Quiz: William Shakespeare
Form Title: William Shakespeare Trivia
Form Description: Test your knowledge of William Shakespeare based on the video transcript.

Questions
1. What nickname is William Shakespeare often known by?
   A) The Playwright
   B) The Bard
   C) The Poet
   D) The Dramatist

   Correct Answer: B) The Bard

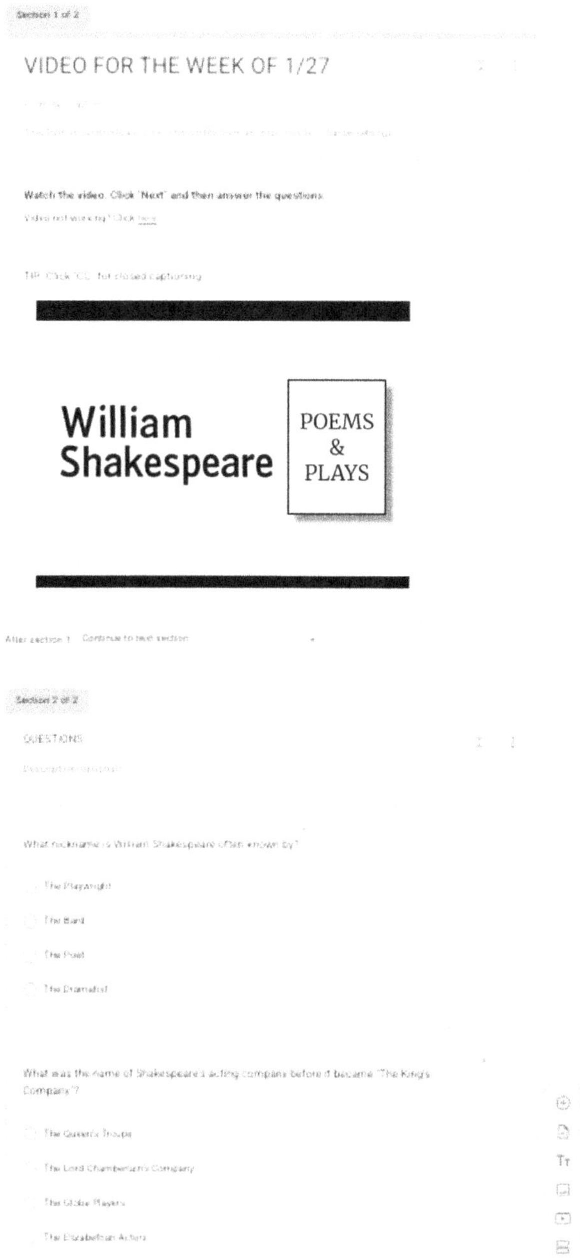

Creating without Limits ♦ 167

FIGURE 8.5 Shakespeare Quiz Form Screenshot

Now you have a self-contained video quiz. If you use only multiple-choice questions, you can set Google Forms to grade it. These quizzes are great for introducing background information or reinforcing past learning. And there's no reason why you can't create your own YouTube videos for the quizzes.

Presentation Defense

Inspired by the grad school thesis defense, the presentation defense adds a twist to the typical public school presentation. A thesis defense in graduate school is a formal oral examination where a student presents and defends their thesis or dissertation research to a committee of faculty members, demonstrating their understanding and mastery of the topic (Birmingham).

Since we're not dealing with graduate students, the presentation defense is less grueling and perhaps more personal. I find that students will be better prepared to explain what they have learned when the crutch of copy/paste and reading from the PowerPoint is removed. This approach may sound like a "gotcha!" but I find it serves to demonstrate a deeper level of understanding.

For example, I used the presentation defense for The Disaster Project, a unit with an objective of research skills. After an engaging video and discussion about the Erfurt Latrine Disaster (Google it!) and the sinking of the USS Indianapolis (with film clips from Jaws!), students chose and researched disasters from history. They could pick from a supplied list of disasters such as the Triangle Shirtwaist Factory Fire, the Aberfan Mine Disaster, and the Exxon Valdez Oil Spill. Students could also choose a disaster that wasn't in the list of 11 suggestions. Students did guide research using supplied graphic organizers and then created a product from a list of choices (more choice!) of things like a newspaper article, a timeline, a movie trailer, and a podcast.

Instead of doing a product showcase and then the reflection, I moved the showcase to the end—after the reflection. That's so that I could use the reflection, which was in the form of a graphic organizer with space to reflect on specific questions. I had students do this structured reflection to facilitate creating a presentation defense question for each student.

The reflection questions were designed to get responses from the students about their process:

	Questions to Answer	Response (2–4 Sentences)
Engagement with Key Questions	What were the most important questions you considered when researching your disaster? How did these questions help you understand the causes, impacts, responses, and legacies of the disaster?	
Process Description	Describe the steps you took to research and create your project. What challenges did you encounter during this process, and how did you overcome them?	
Connection to Research	How did your research influence your understanding of the disaster? In what ways did your research impact the decisions you made when creating your project?	
Critical Thinking	Discuss a different perspective or interpretation of the disaster that you considered during your research. How did this perspective change or influence your own views on the disaster?	
Insight and Learning	What was the most significant thing you learned from completing this project? How has your understanding of the disaster and its impacts changed as a result of this project?	

Student responses allowed me to set up a thread in ChatGPT that worked almost like a factory. With 40 students doing this project, I appreciate that kind of help. When I input the raw material (student reflections), it does its thing and gives me a finished product (presentation defense question). Thus, once set up, I could get a different and personalized defense question for each student based on their project reflection in a very short amount of time.

In this thread, we are going to come up with "defense" questions for showcase presentations. First, I will give you the assignment and rubric. Then you wait for me to upload a student reflection. When I do, create a question. Please base the question on the reflection rather than the assignment prompt and rubric—these are for context only. I'm looking for questions that are meaningful to the student's individual learning/reflection experience. Do that each time I upload a student reflection. The questions need to be simple and straightforward since they will be part of the oral presentation. Does this make sense?

Yes, I understand what you're looking for. You want a specific question for each student that delves deeper into their reflection assignment, aiming to draw out more thoughtful and perhaps less obvious insights that go beyond the basic objectives listed in the rubric. This approach will encourage students to reflect more critically on their own learning process and the content of their project in a way that reveals deeper understanding and personal engagement with the topic.

Then I upload the assignment and rubric. My first student's reflection is on a project they did on the 1919 Great Boston Molasses Flood. See Figure 8.6.

PROJECT REFLECTION

	Questions to Answer	Your Response (2–4 Sentences)
Engagement with Key Questions* *the questions given with the prompt	What were the most important questions you considered when researching your disaster? How did these questions help you understand the causes, impacts, responses, and legacies of the disaster?	The most important questions for me were what caused the disaster and what affects did that have on people. I found that these were the most important parts of the disaster; seeing as the disaster itself was simple. These questions helped me understand the events and place them on a linear timeline. They helped me understand by forcing me to open my mind wider than just the day of the event.
Process Description	Describe the steps you took to research and create your project. What challenges did you encounter during this process, and how did you overcome them?	When researching for this project, I started by just reading one or two reliable sources about this source to get a general understanding. Then I evaluated my research to see what I was missing. My research was pretty inclusive from the start, but I struggled to find sources with new information and perspectives; most of my research was pretty repetitive.
Connection to Research	How did your research influence your understanding of the disaster? In what ways did your research impact the decisions you made when creating your project?	Before doing research, I really didn't know anything about this disaster, so my research formed, my understanding. The information about how much molasses remained after the flood made me want to include molasses in my project, so I glued the pictures on with molasses.
Critical Thinking	Discuss a different perspective or interpretation of the disaster that you considered during your research. How did this perspective change or influence your own views on the disaster?	With this disaster, a lot of the research was in agreement, but there were multiple perspectives about the causes of the tank break. These influenced my perspectives because knowing that there were multiple valid reasons the tank may have broken made me less fond of the company that owned the tank. To me, this means that the tank was poorly designed and the company made mistakes, it wasn't just bad luck.
Insight and Learning	What was the most significant thing you learned from completing this project? How has your understanding of the disaster and its impacts changed as a result of this project?	Before this project, I didn't know anything about this disaster. I really liked learning about where some of our modern building codes/ laws came from. It's important to know where these rules come from to know that they're important to prevent huge disasters.

FIGURE 8.6 Project Reflection Table

Here's the question that ChatGPT came up with:

> Considering the varied perspectives on the causes of the disaster you researched, how did exploring these differing viewpoints affect your approach to presenting the disaster's narrative in your project? Can you discuss how this influenced your choice of materials or presentation style?

I can always put on my differentiation hat if to get the same question but phrased in a way I know my student will respond to better:

> Can you rephrase the question in simpler language?

> How did looking at different reasons for why the disaster happened change the way you decided to show the disaster in your project? Did it make you choose different materials or ways to show your information?

Notice the question about choosing different materials. ChatGPT picked up on the fact that the student used actual molasses instead of glue when constructing the project. That's the kind of detail I want that isn't in the assignment prompt or the rubric. And questions based on students' own reflections reflect learning and understanding rather than some sort of "gotcha":

How did your interest in space as a kid help you decide what to draw for this project, especially the part about kids and families watching the event? How do you think this focus made your drawing tell the story better?

How did considering the factory owners' perspective on safety protocols influence the way you crafted your radio broadcast, and what was your approach to balancing this view with the workers' experiences?

How did your research into the technical failures at Fukushima Daiichi and their consequences influence your opinion on the use of nuclear power, and how did this perspective shape the way you presented the information in your newspaper project?

How did the stories of the survivors influence your approach to presenting the Lituya Bay Megatsunami in your showcase, and what did you find most striking about their experiences?

How did balancing the different portrayals of the Soviet Union's response, from secrecy to heroism, challenge you in writing your newspaper article, and how do you think this balance impacted the overall message of your article?

How did learning about both the bad and good results of the Great Chicago Fire change how you see the event, and how did you show this in your newspaper?

How did learning about the time period of the Hindenburg disaster affect the way you designed your newspaper, and what was the most surprising thing you discovered about how the disaster impacted people?

I suspect the examples in this chapter don't even begin to scratch the surface of the learning techniques and resources that you—the architect—can create using AI. And don't limit your creations to textual ones. There are images and videos and audio and podcasts and just about anything you can think of at your command.

Chapter 8 Postscript: Ethical Considerations

Teachers need to design learning activities with these issues in mind:

- **Authenticity of Student Work:** This chapter emphasizes using AI to create diverse, engaging learning experiences. Educators should ensure that AI tools are used to supplement rather than replace the authentic work of students. This involves creating activities where AI assists in the learning process instead of replacing it (Sackstein; Holcombe and Wozniak).
- **Equity:** Not all students may have equal access to the necessary technology, which could widen the gap in educational opportunities. Schools need to ensure that all students have the resources needed to benefit from AI-enhanced learning. This may include school-provided devices or software that is accessible on various platforms (Devon; Stravopodis).
- **Data Privacy and Student Monitoring:** AI systems often require the collection of personal data to customize learning experiences. Educators and institutions must prioritize student data privacy when implementing AI tools and use systems that comply with data protection laws (Maddux; Soares).
- **Bias in AI Outputs:** AI tools can sometimes produce biased or inaccurate content. Educators should regularly evaluate AI tools to ensure their outputs are accurate and free of biases ("Addressing Bias in AI | Center for Teaching Excellence"; "AI Biases Explained—Learn More about Them").

Learning with AI. On Their Terms

The possibilities to create and revise engaging ways to learn are endless and only limited by your vision and creativity. It is important to keep informed of advances in technology, especially a hyper-rapidly advancing one like AI. Because things move so quickly, a list of URLs in this book would be outdated before publication. So be your own list-maker. Form partnerships with other educators at your school and online. Subscribe to newsletters like The Rundown AI (www.therundown.ai) for consistently current and updated curated content. Google and search and read. Try stuff in your classroom (and tell your students that you're trying something new—they'll be happy to tell you what works and what doesn't).

Be a lifelong learner. Be a lifelong experimenter. Being afraid to fail is being afraid to learn.

As educators, we have the unique opportunity to guide students in using AI ethically and effectively. This means teaching them how to write meaningful prompts, evaluate outputs critically, and reflect on the role AI plays in their learning. These skills not only enhance classroom learning but also prepare students to use AI responsibly and confidently in their future endeavors. With intentional integration, AI can support all of this while helping us reimagine what's possible in education.

Ultimately, the AI-infused classroom isn't about the technology itself—it's about the students. If you take away anything at all from reading this book, take John Warner's question: "Why make students do something that an algorithm can do?" (Juliani). If nothing else, make sure the assignments, activities, and tasks you ask your students to do are genuinely human ones. AI is a tool, but the focus remains on the learner: their curiosity, their growth, their creativity, and their ability to think deeply and independently.

Works Cited

"Addressing Bias in AI | Center for Teaching Excellence." *Center for Teaching Excellence*, The University of Kansas, 2025, https://cte.ku.edu/addressing-bias-ai.

"AI Biases Explained—Learn More about Them." *Covisian*, 24 June 2024, https://covisian.com/tech-post/ai-biases-explained-learn-more-about-them/.

Birmingham, Alison. "What Is a Thesis Defense?" Graduate Programs for Educators, n.d., https://www.graduateprogram.org/blog/what-is-a-thesis-defense/.

"Constructivism in Education." *UBC Master of Educational Technology Program*, 2015, https://constructivism512.weebly.com/meet-the-theorists.html.

Devon, Joe. "The Impact of AI in Advancing Accessibility for Learners with Disabilities." *EDUCAUSE Review*, 10 Sept. 2024, https://er.educause.edu/articles/2024/9/the-impact-of-ai-in-advancing-accessibility-for-learners-with-disabilities.

Holcombe, Amy, and Steve Wozniak. "Using AI to Fuel Engagement and Active Learning." *ASCD*, 1 July 2024, https://ascd.org/el/articles/using-ai-to-fuel-engagement-and-active-learning.

Juliani, A. J. "Teaching and Learning in the AI Age with John Warner." *A. J. Juliani*, 2022, https://www.ajjuliani.com/videos-essays/v/monday-morning-flow-c5f9z-2lrkb.

Maddux, Christopher. "The Importance of Student Data Privacy." *Education Technology Insights*, https://stem.educationtechnologyinsights.com/cxoinsights/the-importance-of-student-data-privacy-nid-2435.html.

Main, Paul. "Cognitive Load Theory: A Teacher's Guide." *Structural Learning*, 17 Jan. 2022, https://www.structural-learning.com/post/cognitive-load-theory-a-teachers-guide.

Sackstein, Starr. "How to Use AI to Enhance, Not Replace, Real Student Learning." *Kappan Online*, 18 Nov. 2024, https://kappanonline.org/ai-enhance-learning/.

"SAMR Model: A Practical Guide for K-12 Classroom Technology Integration." *PowerSchool*, 13 Apr. 2021, https://www.powerschool.com/blog/samr-model-a-practical-guide-for-k-12-classroom-technology-integration/.

Soares, Wellington. "AI Platform Use by Teachers Leads to Student Privacy Worries." *Chalkbeat*, 13 Dec. 2024, https://www.chalkbeat.org/2024/12/13/ai-tools-used-by-teachers-can-put-student-privacy-and-data-at-risk/.

Stravopodis, Minas. "AI and Access to Education: Bridging the Digital Divide." *IRIS Sustainable Development*, 7 Mar. 2024, https://www.irissd.org/post/ai-and-access-to-education-bridging-the-digital-divide.

"The TPACK Framework Explained (with Classroom Examples)." *PowerSchool*, 20 Apr. 2022, https://www.powerschool.com/blog/the-tpack-framework-explained-with-classroom-examples/.

Tomlinson, Carol Ann. "What Is Differentiated Instruction?" *Reading Rockets*, WETA, 2025, https://www.readingrockets.org/topics/differentiated-instruction/articles/what-differentiated-instruction.

"Universal Design for Learning | Accessibility Resources at UNCG." *Accessibility Resources at UNCG*, 2025, https://accessibility.uncg.edu/for-all/udl/.

"What Is Experiential Learning?" *Institute for Experiential Learning*, 2025, https://experientiallearninginstitute.org/what-is-experiential-learning/.

Appendix A

The table categorizes ways students can constructively use artificial intelligence (AI) as an educational tool. Example prompts use the objective-details-request format discussed in Chapter 2. You'll notice the example prompts refer to student-created/supplied information. This keeps the student as the curator of the information and the originator of the work.

Category	Task	Description	Example Prompt a Student Might Use
Organizing and Synthesizing	Organizing Student Notes	Students upload handwritten or typed notes, brainstorming lists, or research findings. ChatGPT organizes the raw information into meaningful categories or themes.	"I need help with a project on the Civil Rights Movement. Can you organize these notes into social, political, and economic impacts? I'm looking for a step-by-step guide on how to sort and present these categories clearly, using straightforward language."
	Graphic Organizer Creation and Topic Narrowing	Students provide a list of topics or questions they're considering and upload notes or a text summary. ChatGPT narrows the topics to the most relevant two to three and suggests a graphic organizer to visualize connections.	"Here are topics and my notes from 'Born A Crime.' I need help narrowing these down to the two or three most relevant topics. Could you also suggest a graphic organizer to visualize the connections between these topics? I'm looking for a simple guide on how to do this, using clear and straightforward language."
	Evidence Synthesis	Students upload selected quotes, textual evidence, or other resources. ChatGPT helps identify connections, patterns, or overarching themes.	"I need help identifying connections, patterns, or overarching themes found in the following quotes and resources on biodiversity and deforestation. Can you summarize the relationship between biodiversity and deforestation using this information? I'm looking for a clear and straightforward explanation."
	Study Guide Creation	Students upload class notes, readings, or study questions. ChatGPT synthesizes the content into a clear, concise study guide.	"I need help synthesizing the following notes and study questions on World War II into a clear, concise study guide. Can you organize this information and guide me on how to structure the study guide effectively? I'm looking for simple and nontechnical language."

(Continued)

Category	Task	Description	Example Prompt a Student Might Use
Exploring and Expanding Ideas	Topic Exploration	Students brainstorm broad topics or research questions for a project or essay, using ChatGPT to expand their ideas.	"I'm brainstorming the following ideas for a project on teen mental health and need help expanding my thoughts. Can you provide some key issues related to these topics? I'm looking for detailed insights to guide my research and project development, using clear and straightforward language."
	Creative Output Brainstorming	Students ask ChatGPT to suggest creative ways to represent their learning in visual, multimedia, or artistic formats.	"I'm working on a research project about the Industrial Revolution and need help brainstorming creative ways to present my findings. Can you suggest some visual, multimedia, or artistic formats that I could use? I'm looking for detailed options that will effectively showcase the information in an engaging way, using clear and straightforward language."
Planning and Execution	Outlining Steps for a Task	Students use ChatGPT to create step-by-step plans for completing assignments based on their input or initial ideas.	"I'm planning the following three-course meal and need help creating a checklist for preparing and plating each dish. Can you provide a step-by-step guide based on the meal plan I've input? I'm looking for clear instructions that outline each task in a straightforward way."
	Writing Scripts for Videos or Presentations	Students upload research notes, outlines, or ideas, and ChatGPT helps turn them into a coherent script.	"I've uploaded my research notes and ideas for an Ethical Considerations project and need help turning them into a coherent script for a 'choose-your-own-adventure' story using Google Slides with non-sequential linking. Can you guide me through creating this script in a clear and straightforward manner?"

(Continued)

Category	Task	Description	Example Prompt a Student Might Use
Analyzing and Building Understanding	Analyzing Student-Collected Data	Students upload spreadsheets, surveys, or experimental data they've collected. ChatGPT identifies trends, patterns, or anomalies in its findings.	"I've uploaded a spreadsheet from my experiment on plant growth under different light conditions and need help analyzing it. Can you identify any trends, patterns, or anomalies in the data? I'm looking for a clear explanation of the findings using straightforward language."
	Vocabulary and Concept Building	Students upload a list of terms or concepts they need to understand, and ChatGPT generates definitions, explanations, or examples.	"I need help understanding the following list of terms related to cellular respiration. Can you provide definitions, explanations, and examples? I'm looking for clear and straightforward explanations to help grasp these concepts effectively."
Providing Feedback	Peer Feedback Simulation	Students upload their draft work, and ChatGPT simulates feedback, providing suggestions for improvement.	"Attached is my storyboard for a short film, and I need simulated peer feedback. Can you provide suggestions for improvement? I'm looking for detailed feedback that helps enhance my storyboard, using clear and straightforward language."

Appendix B

Below, you will find the text of the first prompt for the unit planning in Chapter 7. To make it easier for you to copy and paste the prompt or to make any modifications toward planning your own units, you can also find a downloadable version of the text in the "Support Material" tab of this book's webpage (www.routledge.com/9781041160830).

In this thread, you'll help me develop a unit called "AI UNIT."

Below are the lesson design and unit structure frameworks. We will use these frameworks.

I will upload ideas and materials and text with an explanation of what it is. When I upload something, you do not need to do anything but acknowledge it; it is a resource for you. Unless/until I ask you to do or create anything, an acknowledgment is fine. Does this make sense?

Universal Patterns for Lesson Design

Engaging Inputs:

Every unit starts with rich, engaging content (e.g., literature, multimedia, or concepts like grief).
Inputs are scaffolded to ensure accessibility, offering students a variety of ways to engage with the material (e.g., videos, texts, simulations).
Universal Principle: Start with engaging, diverse materials that establish context and provoke curiosity.

Process Filters:

Tasks like note-taking, evidence gathering, and thematic connections act as filters. These require active student involvement and prevent simple regurgitation of AI outputs.

Filters Emphasize:

Personalization: Students must reframe or reinterpret content in their own words.

Collaboration: Teams work together on interpretations or creative outputs.

Universal Principle: Build checkpoints that require students to engage deeply, personalize their learning, and collaborate meaningfully.

Creative Outputs:

Each unit includes a tangible product requiring creativity, analysis, or synthesis (e.g., essays, videos, artworks).

Outputs are multimodal, allowing for diverse student strengths while showcasing original thinking.

Universal Principle: Culminate learning in an original, multimodal product that cannot be outsourced to AI.

Reflection:

Reflections: Students analyze their processes and learning, often addressing how they used tools like AI.

Peer Review or Presentations: Sharing their work fosters accountability and builds communication skills.

Universal Principle: Include reflective and evaluative steps that ensure students internalize their learning and validate their effort.

AI Integration:

AI is positioned as a supportive tool rather than a replacement, emphasizing critical thinking and human oversight.

Tasks are designed so AI augments the process (e.g., generating prompts or organizing ideas) while requiring students to refine or apply the outputs creatively.
Universal Principle: Use AI as a tool for scaffolding, emphasizing that students evaluate, refine, and own the final output.

Unit Structure Templates: Textual Descriptions and Use Cases

Linear:

Best for: Content-heavy units or sequential learning.
Ideal for: Teaching step-by-step procedures, vocabulary acquisition, or foundational skills in any subject.
Can also work well for: Units where mastering each step builds toward the next.
Questions to Consider: Is the unit content-heavy or sequential, requiring mastery of specific steps? Does the material include procedures or rote learning (e.g., math facts or lab safety)?

Branching Pathways:

Best for: Units that prioritize flexibility, differentiation, or student choice.
Ideal for: Accommodating diverse learning styles, skill levels, or interests.
Effective for: Offering multiple approaches to the same goal or allowing students to evaluate different methods.
Questions to Consider: Do you want to offer flexibility in how students achieve objectives? Do students have diverse skills, preferences, or learning needs? Do you need to provide accommodations for learning disabilities? Do you want students to explore multiple methods?

Cycle:

Best for: Refining and improving work through trial, feedback, and revision.

Works in: STEM or project-based learning, as well as creative disciplines like art or writing.

Ideal for: Skill mastery through multiple drafts, testing, or iterative practice.

Questions to Consider: Do you want students to refine skills through repeated attempts and feedback? Is the focus on improving outcomes through trial and revision? Do you want to provide structured opportunities to address mistakes and build confidence?

Hybrid:

Best for: Combining teamwork and individual accountability.

Ideal for: Big projects that benefit from both branching pathways and cycles.

Effective for: Gamifying learning with collaborative tasks balanced by personal responsibility.

Suitable for: Interdisciplinary projects.

Questions to Consider: Do students need to collaborate while also demonstrating individual skills? Does the project require both flexibility and refinement through cycles? Is the unit well-suited to combining teamwork with independent accountability?

Index

A

AI
  as assistant, *see* AI, as collaborative partner
  as collaborative partner 19, 110, 151, 156–157; *see also* AI, ethics
  as creative partner, *see* AI, as collaborative partner
  as organizational support 19, 22, 97, 179
  as scaffold 50; *see also* Scaffolding
  as supportive tool 35
  brainstorming with 50
  copy/paste 2
    misuse 12
  definition of AI 8
  disruption of education 2
  errors 26
  ethics 29, 55, 71, 87, 105, 152, 174
    adaptability 72
    authenticity of student work 174
    bias 56, 105, 174
    data security 29, 55, 106, 174
  environmental impact 56
  errors generated by AI 152
  equity of access 29, 71, 87, 105, 152, 174
  human interaction 87
  implicit bias 88
  job market concerns 56
  learning autonomy 72
  scaffolding concerns 87
  support as crutch 29, 105, 152
  generative definition of AI 9
  integration into learning activities 50
  organizing with 50
  refining ideas with 50
  tools 19
  visual supports 97

Algorithmic vs human tasks 9–10
Assessment
  authentic assessment 34
  limitations of traditional assessment 11
  Quiz of Understanding 130
  rubric creation with AI 125
  YouTube quiz 165
Authentic learning 34

B

Blank canvas approach 36
Bloom's Taxonomy 60
Branching pathways model 63, 69, 78, 79
  alternative pathways 62–63, 69

C

Career relevance 35, 98
Choosing a model 77
Cognitive load 18, 29, 92, 110, 156
Collaboration 41, 69, 70
Completion culture 11
Constructive alignment 34
Constructivism 17, 59, 75, 91, 109, 155
Content in different forms 161
Creative challenge 36
Creative output 38, 42, 45, 52, 54, 55, 60, 61, 63, 85, 112, 133
  rubric 44
Curiosity 39
Cycle model 64, 70, 78, 81

D

Data security, *see* AI, ethics, data security
Differentiated instruction 33, 60, 75, 91, 95, 109, 155

E

Education system flaws 10–11
Engagement 99
Engaging input 38, 39, 50, 53, 54, 60, 71, 116, 161
Equity, *see* AI, ethics, equity of access
Evidence gathering 41
Experiential learning 18, 33–34, 76, 92, 155–156

F

Feedback
  and practice 98
  providing 182
Five-stage Framework 38
Formative assessment 60

G

Grading, *see* Weighting of the stages
Grecian Urn problem 35–36
Group roles 97

H

Human creativity 34
Hybrid model 65, 70, 78, 83

I

Internalizing learning 47
Iteration 71

J

Job preparation, *see* Career relevance

L

Learning design
  need for change 11
Lesson planning with AI 113, 183
Linear model 61, 68, 77

M

Meaningful work 35
Metacognition 34, 60
Mini-presentations 158
Modeling, *see* Simulation/modeling
Mystery-based engagement 39–40

N

Note organization 22
Note-taking 41

O

Organizing and synthesizing 180

P

Pathways, *see* Branching pathways model
Pandemic teaching lessons 1
Pedagogical intent 93–94
Peer evaluation 46–47
Personalization 41
Personalized questions 169
Practice, *see* Feedback, and practice
Practical considerations 98
Presentation defense 168
Process filter 38, 41, 51, 54, 60, 61, 112, 120, 164
Project-based learning 33, 35, 76
Prompt
  effectiveness 23
  engineering 23–24
  template 23–24

R

Reflection 38, 47, 55, 60, 61, 63, 71, 102, 112, 141, 169
Revision cycles, *see* Cycle model

S

SAMR model 92, 110, 156
Scaffolding 65
Self-regulated learning 18
Shortcuts in learning 2, 11
Showcase 45–46
Simulation/modeling 97
Social constructivism 17
Student-centered learning 35
Student choice 43

Student needs 95
Student thinking 25
Study guide 22
Synthesizing, *see* Organizing and synthesizing

T

Teaching purpose 11
Technology, fear of 2, 5
TPACK framework 18, 92, 110, 156

U

Universal Design for Learning 59, 76, 156

Unit models
 branching pathways, *see* Branching pathways model
 cycle, *see* Cycle model
 hybrid, *see* Hybrid model
 linear, *see* Linear model

W

Weighting of the stages 52–53

Z

Zone of proximal development 18, 75–76, 91, 109–110

For Product Safety Concerns and Information please contact our EU
representative GPSR@taylorandfrancis.com
Taylor & Francis Verlag GmbH, Kaufingerstraße 24, 80331 München, Germany

www.ingramcontent.com/pod-product-compliance
Lightning Source LLC
Chambersburg PA
CBHW061447300426
44114CB00014B/1875